All over the country, Country Folk
have said, and incomers have heard,

"You ain't from here, are ya?"

Other Books by this Author

Fiction

The Double Cousins and the Mystery of the Missing Watch
     WinePress Publishing, 2009 (now out of business)
     (New ISBN assigned by Horse Shoe Press, 2015)

The Double Cousins and the Mystery of the Torn Map
     Ambassador International, 2011

The Double Cousins and the Rushmore Treasure
     Ambassador International, 2014

The Double Cousins and the Mystery of Custer's Gold
     Ambassador International, coming Fall of 2015

The Nearly Twins and the Secret in the Mason Jar
     Ambassador International, coming Spring of 2016

Non-Fiction

All I Have Needed: A Legacy for Life
     Ambassador International, 2013

You Ain't From Here, Are Ya?

Reflections on Southern Culture from an Outsider

— BEING —

A Year of Observations for the *Newberry Observer*, Newberry, South Carolina

Miriam Jones Bradley

Published by Horse Shoe Press
P. O. Box 673, Horse Shoe, NC 28742

Library of Congress Control Number: 2015908355

Publisher's Cataloging-in-Publication data

Bradley, Miriam Jones.
You ain't from around here, are ya? : reflections on southern culture by an outsider - being a year of observations for the Newberry Observer, Newberry, South Carolina / by Miriam Jones Bradley. – Horse Shoe, NC., Horse Shoe Publications, 2015. – 1st ed.
pages cm
Includes index
ISBN-13: 978-1-943556-01-4
ISBN-10: 1-943556-01-6
1. Journalism--Cross-cultural studies. 2. Journalism – Biographical. 3. Journalism – Anecdotes. 4. Southern States – Anecdotes. 5. Southern States – Social life and customs. I. Title.
HM621-656
394

DEDICATION

To those who have gone before: Western, Southern, and Unknown. Your "hand-me-downs" of custom, tradition, and habit clothe us in much of what makes us recognizable to ourselves and to those around us;

And to that little part of ourselves that came into being in Newberry and remains there forever.

CONTENTS

ACKNOWLEDGEMENTS

Acknowledging everyone we should for a book such as this would read like a phone book of Newberry, plus an exhaustive list of family and friends elsewhere. That being said, here are some of the individuals and groups that we feel deserve particular mention:

Leslie Moses and the staff at the *Newberry Observer*, without whom there would, of course, have been no weekly newspaper column;

Randy Berry and the staff at *Books on Main*, who were almost as instrumental in the project as the newspaper itself;

Friends and coworkers at Newberry County Memorial Hospital and Lexington Medical Center, who are sometimes quoted shamelessly and entirely without proper attribution, and who in so many ways provided education in Southern Culture as well as encouragement in the writing process;

Orrie and Mona Perrell, who "adopted" us and welcomed us into their lives;

Pastor and Mrs. David Clark and our church family at Lighthouse Baptist Church, who were unfailing in their encouragement and support;

The writers group of Newberry, who provided not only encouragement but also valuable suggestions and constructive criticism;

Miriam's niece, Megan, who applied her Library Science course on Cataloging to help us create the Publisher's Cataloging-in-Publication block;

Miriam Jones Bradley

To these, and to so many more, our heartfelt thanks.

— 0 —
Introduction

These pieces are from my weekly column in the *Newberry Observer*, Newberry, South Carolina, which ran from June 2010 through August 2011. They are arranged here, more or less, in the order in which they appeared in the newspaper.

This book is both a response to several suggestions and/or requests for a collection of these columns and a way of reminding ourselves of the good memories we have from Newberry. It also serves (well, we hope) as a thank-you and note of appreciation and affection to our friends and coworkers, indeed all the residents of Newberry, South Carolina — "like 'Mayberry', but new".

That is one reason that we felt we *must* include an image specific to Newberry — and nowhere else — on the cover where we were trying to evoke the idea of "Southern". The picture of the Old Courthouse serves that purpose very well, indeed.

Magnolias

A magnolia is featured on the cover for a couple of reasons: long before I moved South and even before I knew it was a Southern flower and symbol, I loved magnolias and had several pieces with pictures of magnolias on them — pictures, a favorite teapot, and so on.

I was therefore *very* pleased to find a large magnolia tree in the side yard of the house in Newberry. We thought we had taken pictures of its huge, beautiful blossoms, but, if so, we could not find them, so we had to use a generic picture.

In any case, it is entirely appropriate to have a picture of a beautiful magnolia blossom on the cover of this book, with all its lovely associations.

Drayton Hall

Drayton Hall is on the cover because it was our favorite South Carolina "touristy" thing to do. I joined the National Historic Trust the first time I visited and it was close enough to Newberry that any out-of-town visitor who was staying long enough was taken to see Drayton Hall.

— Miriam Jones Bradley
Hendersonville, NC
January 2015

Miriam's byline & photo – introducing her to Newberry readers

—1—
My Introduction to Newberry

The first time we drove into Newberry I knew. This was a real place, one I could call home.

We sailed past the general business area of Highway 34 with its mix of national chain stores and hometown businesses. Once we hit the residential area of Main Street, we slowed, not wanting to miss anything. These were unique, marvelous homes, some very old. I like old.

Then we arrived in downtown Newberry with its crown jewel, the town square with a real honest-to-goodness opera house. Oh my. I knew this was my kind of place. For a South Dakota girl living in South Florida, this was as good as it could get.

If I ever build a town from scratch, I'll start with a town square, one with a park in the middle surrounded by brick streets. If you have one of those, the people and stores will come. It provides a core to your town that nothing else can.

It also reminds me of Broken Bow, the small town in central Nebraska near where my grandparents ranched and where they lived after retirement. It's the town where the Joneses still gather every other year on the first weekend in August. Broken Bow has been my heart's home my entire life.

I like to say I've lived from sea to shining sea, California to Florida, but mostly I lived in the Great Plains, specifically Nebraska, Wyoming and South Dakota. I've learned first-hand that there are great differences among areas of our country. The culture in South Dakota is much different than that in South Florida. Oh wait—there is no underlying culture in South Florida, anything that ties together the whole community.

My point is, when you move, you have to be ready to adjust, assimilate, and acknowledge that you may never, ever arrive. You may never be a local, and that's all right.

I've been the new kid in town, and I've watched others struggle with learning a new culture. There is a special balance required. It all comes down to respect and humor.

You must respect the fact that you are not going to change this culture. You have to recognize that it may change you, even if it's only small changes.

Embrace what you can, acknowledge what you can't, and just be yourself. Above all, don't forget to laugh about it. Some of the world's best humor comes from our differences.

In this column I plan to share my impressions of southern culture. I can only do this from my perspective for it's the only one I have and it's not Southern. It's not Northern either. It's Western and we tend to say things how we see them.

So just run all I say through the "she's not from here, bless her heart" filter and know this one thing—I haven't changed my mind about Newberry. My first impression was dead-on: This place is real and it's a place I can call home.

Southern culture as seen from the outside looking in

The headline of Miriam's first column in the Newberry Observer

−2−

Southern Politeness

I noticed it first at Wal-Mart. People stopped and waited to let you go first when the aisle was crowded instead of barreling right through. It was a kind deference that was the complete opposite of a visit to Wal-Mart in South Florida where, as my husband likes to say, "they'd as soon run you down as look at you."

"She said 'excuse me'," I whispered to my husband. I'm sure my mouth was open, jaw sagging.

"This is the South, Miriam. People are polite here."

He was right. Polite is one of the top five words I would use to describe the people of the South. It's an inbred decency, a deference to others that makes a difficult situation a little easier. It's often demonstrated with two phrases used when broaching a difficult subject. Either people lead off with, "I don't mean to be ugly," or end with, "well, bless her heart" – maybe both.

The people out west are a bit more direct. They are polite too, only in a more subtle way. Their politeness is less verbal and they don't use the nice phrases to soften what they are thinking, They are more likely just to say it. If they can't bring themselves to say it outright, they are apt to be like my Grandma and say nothing at all.

I am spontaneous and direct and can come across in a tense moment as too blunt. I've seen it in the faces of those I interact with, that moment I cross the invisible line. This is probably why my aunt who has lived in Athens, Georgia, most of her married life felt the need to give me this hint when she heard I was moving here. "Miriam, you can say pretty much whatever you need to say about someone as long as you end it with, 'well, bless her heart.'"

I thought she was kidding, since we are a family heavy on the humor, but I soon found out she was dead serious.

I sometimes don't know how to take Southern politeness. I wonder if there is sarcasm under that smile. I wish a person would come out and say what they think so I don't have to try and figure out how sincere they are.

Most of the time, though, I can't help but think that a basic culture of being polite no matter what difficult person or situation you face can hardly be bad. It seems like most of our world needs a little more of this Southern trait.

I don't know which way is better, the Western or Southern. The safest choice, I'm sure is to follow the Bible principle my Daddy taught me and "speak the truth in love."

— 3 —

Southernisms 101

I was only half listening to the conversation, so at first I thought I had misunderstood when my coworker said, "She sure enough showed out last night."

"She what?" I asked, perplexed.

"She showed out last night," my co-worker repeated.

My befuddled mind searched for a possible meaning. She showed out? What does that mean?

"What did she show out," I asked. I could feel my eyebrows climbing toward the top of my head.

Now it was my coworker's turn to look confused. "She acted out," she explained.

Understanding dawned. "Oh! She threw a temper tantrum!"

I had been stymied by another Southernism.

This scenario isn't unusual for me. The difference between Southern and Western accents is challenging enough, but with the occasional Southernism thrown in, it can lead to confusion, comedy, or both.

One of the most confusing sets of phrases for me is the cut off-cut on pair. While I had never heard "cut off the lights" the concept was reasonable. If you flip the switch or turn off the light it cuts the electricity so "cut off the lights" makes sense. However, "cut the lights on" makes no sense at all to me! If you are cutting the power how can you expect it to come back on? It's just a literalist thing, I guess.

Another one that makes me chuckle is, "I'm going to carry Grandma to the store today." In my mind's eye I see Grandma either on the person's back or in his arms being carried into the grocery store.

Ah, the grocery store. That reminds me of another one, the "buggy". Out west a buggy is an old-fashioned mode of transportation or something you push a baby in. The cart at the store is called, boring as it may seem, a grocery cart.

Besides "bless her heart," my favorite Southernism is the phrase that's used when words won't do. "Mmm mmm MMM MMM mmm!" That has to be the most useful Southernism ever invented.

My husband also tells me not to try talking with a southern accent. He says I'm not very good at it, and it's painful to listen to. I think he's right because whenever I try, I see the same pained expression on other faces that he gets on his.

When I went home to South Dakota my niece informed me, "you are starting to sound like those cousins that came to visit from down South." This surprised me since I'm sure I don't have an accent. Then I realized, it's the phrases I'm picking up.

The Southernisms. Like "bless her heart," "y'all," and don't be telling me that".

They're contagious, you see, and so I told my thirteen year old nephew, "Now don't y'all be going and doing any growing while I'm gone. I don't want to come back here and find you grew six inches and your voice has done changed. Don't be doing that to me now, you hear? If you do I just might have to show out a bit."

— 4 —

Southern Sweet Tea

A couple of years ago my sister came to visit. After picking her up at the airport in Charlotte we swung through the drive-through at McDonald's to get something to eat. She ordered a burger and an iced tea. As I pulled away she took a big swig of the tea and choked, gagged, and spluttered. Then she looked at me accusingly, with indignation in her eyes, and said, "This tea is sweet!" She choked and gagged some more and set the tea down in the cup carrier. " I can't drink this. It's too sweet."

While laughing, I apologized. I hadn't even thought to warn her.

Tea is one thing that is extremely different here. Most people out west don't sweeten their tea at all. Our Mom added enough sugar so that it was slightly sweetened. Her recipe was one-quarter cup of sugar per gallon of tea. Yep, you read it right. She put in just enough sugar to barely be noticed. If you wanted more you could add it yourself; the sugar bowl was generally in the middle of the table.

One summer when we were visiting our Grandparents' ranch in Nebraska, the hired man captured the attention of every child at the table. Each time he poured a glass of tea, he would add six or seven teaspoons of sugar and then stir, and stir, and stir. We couldn't believe our eyes. It so impressed me that this action made it into my children's mystery based on our summer visits to the ranch. The thought that people would drink their tea that sweet . . .

Since coming to Newberry I've come to enjoy sweet tea, as long as it isn't too sweet. My preference is to mix the sweet tea half and half with unsweetened. Then it's about right. Occasionally though, when I'm very thirsty I just want unsweetened tea, no sugar. I find it quenches my thirst better.

The other day I went through McDonald's drive-through again, this time alone. I asked for an unsweetened iced tea. After a short silence, the employee asked me to repeat the request.

"Could I have an unsweetened iced tea, please?" I asked again.

Another silence followed by this question, spoken in utter disbelief. "Do you want sweet tea without the sugar?"

"Yes, ma'am," I said. "I do."

I imagined her inside the store shaking her head and saying, "She's not from around here, bless her heart."

Oh, and my sister? After being here for several weeks she developed a tolerance for sweetened tea. In fact, a few days after she returned to Colorado, she called me. "I sure could use a good glass of sweet tea. But it's just not the same out here!"

[Miriam's husband, The Southerner, is not impressed with "Nebraska Sweet Tea", which tends to be weak and hardly sweet.

His mama's recipe for making a gallon of Southern sweet tea was to boil the teabags (4 family size or quart teabags or 16-20 regular size teabags) in about a quart of water and then let them steep, rather than just pouring boiling water over them before steeping. Boiling the teabags produces a stronger, more bitter brew that stands up to ice cubes. Add 1 cup (more or less, to taste) sugar to the jug or pitcher, pour the hot tea over the sugar to dissolve it, (squeeze the teabags to get all the "goody" out of them if you want) and fill the jug with cold water.]

— 5 —
In Praise of Porches

As always when in North Carolina, I am starting my morning with coffee on the porch. In the winter I'll huddle inside a blanket, only my hand poking out to hold the hot coffee cup. When I'm too cold to stand it anymore, I hurry back inside.

In the summer I watch and listen to the birds, the roosters, the dogs, and, I suspect, a pig up the road. We have five lots so I can sit on my porch and see across the yard and y'all know how much I love my space.

Sometimes I spend most of the day on the porch, writing.

I blame this porch on Newberry. Yep, that's right. Newberry. Oh, it's not that I had never experienced the loveliness of a porch. I have had an unrequited love for porches for quite a few years.

I grew up in a neighborhood much like many in Newberry, some huge houses, some medium sized, some with big porches meant to live on, and some with the functional three steps and a spot to stand while waiting for the door to open. Ours was the latter.

When we moved away, it was to more modern houses which didn't appreciate the need for a porch you could sit on. I guess no one used them, so they quit building them, kind of like formal dining rooms now.

But still, there was my Grandparents' porch. When they moved into town after selling the ranch in '83, they bought a small house with a small porch. There was room for two of those metal porch chairs in the corner. Grandma grew her flowers in pots along the edge, and she and Grandpa sat and enjoyed watching the neighbors walk and drive by. Of course, living in Central Nebraska, this only lasted about six months of the year.

If they knew you were coming they would be sitting on the porch waiting.

To my great sadness, the house we bought in Newberry lacked one thing . . . a porch. It was perfect in every other way, so I tried to satisfy my porch need by gazing at other people's porches as I walked around Newberry. We also bought a swing for the yard in Newberry hoping it would help.

These however, were simply Band-Aids. I was surrounded by porches and I needed my own.

So, when we determined to update my husband's family home outside Hendersonville, I told him I wanted a porch. I needed a porch. I really believed I must have a porch. He wasn't unwilling, but it did seem an extravagance.

We had the porch built and the difference in the house is amazing, so much more inviting and hospitable. We enjoy the extra space too. And guess what, we are talking about someday building an enclosed porch on the side of the house.

So from my porch in North Carolina to you, "Thank you, Newberry!"

Newberry's "Pork in the Park", April 2008.
The back of the 1852 Old Courthouse is in the background.

— 6 —

Barbecue – Pork or Beef?

My husband says that, for me, if it didn't moo it's not meat. I tell him that's not exactly true. I'll also eat it if it clucked or oinked, but not if it sucked its cheeks in and out and swam. With a few exceptions, I don't really care for fish. I guess it's because there just aren't many oceans around South Dakota and Nebraska.

Last week we had our Jones Family reunion in Broken Bow, Nebraska, where beef rules supreme. Oh, they do have hogs in the area. In fact, my uncle and cousin have a hog barn on their ranch, but the primary crop there in central Nebraska is beef. The reunion is usually heavy on the beef with some chicken thrown in for variety. Hamburgers, sloppy joes, barbeque beef sandwiches — you get the picture.

Imagine my surprise when Mom called a few months ago and said she and my aunt were planning Pulled Pork Sandwiches for the meal our families are responsible to prepare. Pulled Pork? Where on earth did they get that idea? I had never eaten pulled pork before coming to South Carolina. BBQ always involved beef or chicken. She continued to add to my confusion when she said we would have coleslaw and peach cobbler. Hmm. Sounded like it was adding up to one great Southern meal.

I jumped on the bandwagon and offered to bring some South Carolina mustard based BBQ sauce, and they agreed.

So, there I was in my beloved central Nebraska surrounded by family eating one of the most well-known southern meals. The mustard based BBQ wasn't a huge hit, probably something about the fact that it was yellow instead of reddish-brown, but it did lead to several fun conversations about the South. I'm hoping some of my western cousins will come down and visit us so we can show them more Southern Culture.

My cultural senses were righted on Monday when I went to the annual, free community BBQ at the fairgrounds in Broken Bow. Sitting on the ground with my nieces and nephews, I devoured my thin sliced beef BBQ sandwich and thought about the differences between Nebraska and South Carolina. Newberry has *Pork in the Park*, while Nebraska has *Beef in the Bow*.

Community, family, and food: maybe there's not that much difference after all.

The Old Courthouse, front view.

— 7 —

Humidity

This is the time of summer when the word "snow" first crosses my mind. Yep, you saw that right: I said snow. The heat and humidity of August in the South is enough to drive my mind straight to the white stuff. Before I moved here it wasn't until Fall that I started thinking about snow, but not anymore.

It's not just the heat; it's the humidity.

I was chatting with the lady at the McDonald's drive-up window the other night as I waited for the car in front of me to leave. (Yes, I was getting unsweetened ice tea). She leaned out the window and commented. "My it's so hot out here, and humid too." She wasn't going to get any disagreement from me.

I tell people I didn't really know what sweat was until I moved from South Dakota to South Florida. Oh, I know. Ladies don't sweat, they "glow" (out west they "glisten"). But it's a bit difficult to sweetly glow in this weather. And then there's the problem of my glasses fogging over when I go outside. In South Dakota steamed up glasses happens when you go inside in the winter. It really messes with my mind.

Coming from the Great Plains I really didn't have a clue what real humidity was. I do remember a visit to Chattanooga years ago when it started to rain, one of those gentle misty rains. I commented on the rain, and my cousin said, "That's not rain, that's just high humidity!" Could have fooled me.

I just now looked it up on the internet, and the humidity here in Newberry at 5:30 p.m. is 65%. That is not too terrible, actually. The humidity in Rapid City, SD, is 39%. They are probably suffering, since there it is often even less than that at this time of year. In 2001 I drove into Rapid City in July and the temperature was 110 degrees with 5% humidity. It felt like a blast furnace as opposed to the sauna effect here. When we were dating, my husband-to-be laughed at me when I complained about 55% humidity. Now I know why.

I am thankful for one thing, though. Unlike South Florida, in Newberry the seasons do change. It may be hot and humid now, but give it a few weeks and we will be enjoying the most beautiful Fall weather I've seen. In fact the extended colorful season is my favorite part of the year here.

And then I can start dreaming about snow without thinking I'm crazy! Bring on Autumn!

— 8 —
Faith

I am a PK. That means "Preacher's Kid" to those of you who don't know, but since this is the Bible Belt, that's probably not many. My Daddy is a Baptist pastor and has been for most of my life. In fact, he was in Seminary when I was born and is still going strong.

I love church. My week is not complete if I don't go to church Sunday morning, Sunday night, and Wednesday evening. Call me weird but that is who I am. That is my culture.

Because of that I feel comfortable here in the South. Out west people are more private about their faith. They don't speak as freely about their church affiliations. When you pray in a restaurant, you stand out, you are conspicuous. Not here. Here, there is nothing unusual about a table full of people bowing their heads to pray before eating their meal at Ronnie's.

Jesus is a big part of the culture in the South, and I love it.

I love knowing that I can verbalize my faith at work without fear of repercussion. I love seeing so many churches, everywhere you look. I even enjoy driving down the road and saying the names of churches I see out loud. I find it interesting, what people somewhere way back in the past decided to name their church. As a life-long Baptist, I can usually tell the particular brand of Baptist by something in the name, although my husband has introduced me to a few brands I didn't even know existed!

I am thankful that church is a part of my culture. But I have had this recurring concern poking its head up. For instance, when Mr. Jimmie prayed in church last Sunday, I got stuck on his first phrase and, I admit, I didn't hear much else he said. He started like this: "Dear Heavenly Father, thank you for the privilege of coming to You today."

Privilege. He said privilege.

You see, sometimes I wonder. Am I in church because it is my privilege? Am I there because, like Pastor Clark preached last Sunday, the Love of God constrains me? Or am I there because it is my culture? I think I'd rather it be the Love of God thing, wouldn't you?

— 9 —

A Middler

When I moved to Newberry I decided to learn about the history of the area. After all, that's the beginning of understanding a culture. So I marched down to my favorite local bookstore, *Books on Main*, and Randy recommended *Our Fathers' Fields* by James Everett Kibler.

It was amazing. I learned about the South through this story of one specific place in Newberry County and the people who purchased it in 1786, settled it, and lived there for six generations. I learned that I had no clue.

Oh, my education was pretty good. I learned about the South, the economy, slavery, State's Rights, the Civil War, Reconstruction, and carpetbaggers. They covered all of that. But for me to really know something, I have to personalize it. That is what this book did for me. It helped me see that the culture here is shaped by the land, the people, and the events of the past.

There is an interdependence here among the people. It is a balance of living among people who are different, yet the same. There is also an independence here. "Don't tell us how to run our lives" seems to be the motto of a lot of people in the South.

There are a lot of other ironies in the South. People are laid back, yet hard working. They are kind, yet cynical. I guess this comes from the ups-and-downs of the history of the South.

Yesterday I had the privilege of reading *Like No Other Place – The Sandhills of Nebraska* by David A. Owen. It was recommended by my cousin, Gordon Jones, who ranches in the Sandhills.

The Sandhills are my roots. That is where my Grandpa grew up. That is where my Daddy was born in a sod house during the Depression.

According to Owen, it is an area of 20,000 square miles with about 5000 residents. It is the largest stabilized sand dune area in North America and among the four largest on Earth. It is good for cattle ranching. It is not good for farming.

This book is a delightful photo documentary of a man from Connecticut who went to the Sandhills, lived among the people, and learned what it means to be a "Sandhiller". I realized as I read it that, like here in the South, the land and the history have created the culture. The Sandhillers are a result of those. They are resourceful, strong-willed, energetic, self-reliant, and able to tolerate the isolation.

What am I? I don't really know. I never lived in the Sandhills but my Daddy's roots are there. My mother came from Kansas City and Denver before arriving in Nebraska in the middle of high school. My step-mom, who raised me from twelve years old, is from farm people in Nebraska. I have lived from California to Florida but mostly in the middle.

I guess that's what I am, a "Middler". Maybe that is why I enjoy learning about other cultures. The next one I find just might be home!

— 10 —
Villages & Community

I am always a little surprised when I see a manufacturing plant along the highway. When I drive to the airport in Charlotte, I pass several. It isn't something I'm used to seeing since manufacturing plants aren't very common where I come from. I'm also intrigued by the old mill buildings around town here. It makes me sad to see them empty, so I'm thrilled with the news that they are to be repurposed.

I suppose the plants being here makes sense, since the textile plants were placed near the cotton-growing regions.

When we were in Nebraska last month, I did see one manufacturing facility. It was for agricultural equipment. In Nebraska, South Dakota, and Wyoming, the main industry is agriculture. There are sugar beets from which we get our sugar. There are the corn fields that we all like because of corn syrup and the corn fields meant to feed the corn-fed cows in the feed-lots that you smell before you see.

There are amber waves of grain where the wheat is grown for our bread. There are the miles of wide-open spaces that are used for pastures for range cattle and the flat parts which are mowed for hay to feed the cattle in the harsh winters.

When my niece, Megan, was about seven, she popped out with a question as we drove through the Sandhills. There were miles and miles of emptiness with an occasional tree, or more often a windmill standing against the skyline.

"How many acres do you need to pasture one cow?" she asked. After we got over the shock of the fact that she had picked up the ranching "lingo", her mother and I told her we didn't know. But she could ask her Grandpa or his brother Jim, and they would be able to tell her. Cattle ranching is in her blood like the mill villages are in the blood of the people in Newberry.

I've enjoyed learning about the mill towns and mill villages from PBS. It is a way of life that has mostly disappeared. Those people were dependent on the mill, yet they were happy.

They had their basic needs met. They had social opportunities in the village. They had schools. They had food. They had churches.

Here we are, all still striving to keep food on the table, educational opportunities for the children, church life, sport, and social activities going. Are we as happy? I don't know. I think in our drive for bigger and better we have lost some of the good things about those times. Oh, I'm sure it wasn't all good. Nothing is. Community is important, though. We need to be reaching out to the people in our lives, the people around us. I find that in Newberry.

— 11 —
Team Loyalty

I'm not much of a sports fan but I do understand the excitement. In 1970 the Nebraska Cornhuskers won the Big 8 championship. I remember it well because it was the first time I ever saw my mother yell at the television! It was a memorable occasion. I didn't know anyone could get that excited about a ball game. I didn't really get it then and I don't now. I'm more into books, I guess.

I lived in Nebraska for eighteen years of my life. The Cornhuskers are big there. Really big. On a game day the entire state wears red. So yes, I've seen fans go crazy. But I have to say that, around here, there is something above and beyond that.

I have never lived in a state that has two major teams. I can just imagine the joy this must provide in some households. The divided ones, that's what I'm talking about.

For instance, the other evening I was driving to work and I saw an interesting sight. The pickup in front of me had the back window covered with three logos. At the top was this phrase, "A House Divided." The three logos were a Gamecock, the Tar Heels Ram, and the Clemson Tiger.

I just shook my head. Bless their hearts!

I don't have a preference, except my husband did his graduate work at the University of South Carolina, so I give a weak "rah" when they win.

In addition, Clemson played Nebraska last year.

What's a girl to do! We were in Nebraska just before the game and I found this really awesome jacket. It was a Cornhusker jacket. And yes, you guessed it. I wore it to work at the hospital on game day. I know it was cheeky, but seeing the heads swivel was worth it all. And, I admit it. I had to rub it in a little when Nebraska won.

Go Huskers! :p

— 12 —
The Old Mill

This afternoon, after working on a project we both dreaded, my husband and I took the convertible, stopped by Sonic for a diet cherry limeade, and took a drive.

"Let's go find that old mill building they are going to renovate," I suggested. I had poked around town one evening looking for it without success, so I had asked some friends at my writers group for general directions.

Following their directions we found it. Wow, that's a massive building. Amazing!

After watching a documentary on PBS about the mill villages in the South, I have been intrigued with the idea of repurposing the one here in Newberry. It is a piece of local history and I like history. I find old buildings help me visualize the past. I also remember my parents' dismay when the old train depot in North Platte, Nebraska, was torn down overnight.

Without any public announcement or discussion, that beautiful historic building that so many of our World War Two soldiers traveled through was gone. And once it's gone there is no bringing it back. My parents were horrified, and as a young child I watched and learned.

What is the big deal about the mill building? Why should we save it? My husband's comment was something like, "That's going to take a LOT of renovation." It will take a lot of money and resources but personally, I hope it succeeds.

You see, I'm the kind person who likes to learn from history. I'm also the kind of person who really can't visualize what something was like if it has all been replaced with new. I'm a visual learner. So, if you take that big old building down and put a bunch of new houses in its place, I won't be able to picture how it was.

I'm sure there are people who would tell you that the mill village life was wonderful. There was a united community, all working in the same industry. They had homes to live in. They enjoyed social and spiritual activities. They could buy anything they needed right there. It was secure and many people wish they still could live in that culture.

I'm sure there are others who would recite the down-side to such a culture. For instance, what happens to the community when the mill closes? That's true too.

But whether you liked the mill village or not, it is a part of our history. From where I am looking, we need to pay more attention to our history, what worked and what didn't. What's the saying? "All we learn from history is that we don't learn from history."

I think repurposing the old mill building is a magnificent way to hang on to a part of the heritage of this town while providing much needed rental housing for our community. That's how I see it.

— 13 —
Oktoberfest

Where is autumn, anyway? With temperatures still in the 90's I long for a chilly day. I want soup weather.

My family and friends out west have been posting all of their cool weather recipes and activities and it's making me jealous. I'm ready for a Saturday, shivering and baking all day long to warm up the house so I don't have to start the furnace. But no, it looks like we have a few more days of warm weather to contend with.

Maybe Oktoberfest will set things right. I absolutely love Oktoberfest. It is all tied up in my first memories of Newberry. We first arrived in Newberry the middle of August, but by the time our belongings showed up and I started my job at the hospital, it was the end of September. When I saw advertisements for Oktoberfest I was curious. I had never been to an Oktoberfest celebration.

That first year we set out and walked from our house to the downtown area. As we got closer you could feel the excitement rushing down the street and dragging you in. My first strong memory is of the band organ. My husband and I are both musical and we were captivated by that instrument. We stood for some time watching and listening. I had never in my life seen such a thing. My husband pointed out that it was appropriate for Oktoberfest, since it was built in Germany, after all.

On down the street we encountered the Gideon Bible group and I was able to get a New Testament for my nephew. It has been my habit to obtain a Gideon Bible for each of my nieces and nephews when they are about three years old. That year it came from Oktoberfest.

At the bookstore we happened upon my favorite part of Oktoberfest, the author signing at *Books on Main*. I was amazed. I had never seen a book signing with that many authors in one place. There it was, right here in little ol' Newberry! Awesome. I found myself dreaming of the day when my book, a children's mystery, would also be featured at Oktoberfest. Sigh.

I don't remember if I bought anything—or as I like to put it—found something I couldn't live without. But I do know that I found one more reason to love Newberry.

Last year I became not just an observer of Oktoberfest. I became an active participant when my book was—drum-roll here, please—featured at the book signing during Oktoberfest. Oh my. I felt I had arrived.

That may be when I really felt at home here. At least that day I did.

So, in all of this late summer heat, as I dream of soup and baked goods, I hold out for Oktoberfest. It's coming up soon and I'll get to hang out again at *Books on Main* with my friends. Come and see us there. And somewhere in Oktoberfest, you too may find something you can't live without.

— 14 —

Columbus Day Again

I looked at my calendar this morning and noticed that October 11th is Columbus Day. I have fond memories of Columbus Day from grade school. We always did crafts based on Columbus and his three ships. Fall is my favorite time of the year too, and Columbus Day always seemed to kick off the season for me.

Columbus Day doesn't exist everywhere in this country, though. For instance, in South Dakota where I lived and worked for ten years, they don't celebrate Columbus Day. In 1990 the legislature there voted to celebrate it as Native American Day instead. The indigenous people aren't called Indians anymore either; they are Native Americans.

I like to tell people I've lived from sea to shining sea. I was born in California and we moved to Nebraska when I was five. Then, when I was in Junior High School we moved back to California for three years before moving to Wyoming, then Nebraska, then South Dakota. After I married I moved from South Dakota to Florida, then here. So, I've lived a lot of places and been exposed to a lot of ethnic and cultural groups.

My first lessons in cultural tolerance came as a baby, before I can remember, really. I don't remember not knowing this song which I'm sure many of you could sing with me. "Jesus loves the little children, all the children of the world. Red, brown, yellow, black, and white; they are precious in His sight . . ."

My parents ministered to, and were friends with people of every one of those colors, so my cultural background is somewhat diverse. I like to think I'm tolerant. But it irritated me that they went and changed MY holiday, Columbus Day, to something for another group. I wanted to say, "pick your own day, some other day, not ours," but I didn't.

I don't know that this irritation speaks well of me. I don't know that it doesn't. I do know that living among people of other cultures is a balancing act. We have to learn to respect their culture, not let it frighten us or irritate us into stupid statements or acts, and still maintain who we are. That's the challenge.

Of course, here in South Carolina we have our own balancing act. It's one that has been maintained to varying degrees of success throughout American History. According to my sources online, and from those who were born in the South, the culture of the South is a combination of the different peoples and races you find here, a hybrid of cultures carefully maintained by respect for one another.

I don't always understand where those lines of respect are. I sometimes say things that could come across as insensitive. But I have been impressed with the balance I find here in Newberry. I enjoy learning from people who are different from me, yet the same.

And, happy day, I get to celebrate Columbus Day again.

— 15 —

Homecoming

I have noticed announcements in the paper lately that area churches are having their homecoming celebrations. It always makes me stop a second to think before the meaning clicks in my brain. You see, where I come from, a homecoming is the high-school or college celebration usually associated with football. I have taken part in those, but a homecoming at church?

The first time I heard that phrase associated with church, I was completely bewildered. Then someone explained that it is a reunion of people who formerly attended the church, an opportunity for people to get together again. It can also include people whose parents, grandparents, or more remote ancestors attended the church. "Oh, like old home week," I said, reassured.

Now it was my friend's turn to look confused.

Old home week is a phrase I am familiar with, but not one I've ever participated in. Where I've lived they are called, boring though it may sound, reunions. It also might be called a church anniversary celebration, but never a homecoming.

As I thought about this difference, I wondered if it had something to do with the fact that the churches in the South are older than the churches in the Great Plains. After all, this land was settled a long time before the Western States.

Unable to come up with a reason, I resorted to the internet. First, I looked up "old home week" and was surprised to find that it was a tradition that started in New England in the 18th and 19th centuries and involved encouraging former residents to come home for a celebration. I was right about old home week being like a homecoming. However, the time frame shot down the idea that it was because the churches here are older.

When I typed in "homecoming" I got a report on the high school/college homecoming idea with a comment stating that some churches also hold homecoming Sundays, encouraging former members and people who have moved away to come home for a reunion.

So, the truth is that the difference between homecoming and old home week is . . . the Mason-Dixon line? I hope this isn't hard evidence that I'm a Yankee! All I know is that whenever old friends get to see each other again it's a joyous occasion! By whichever name it's called, it's a celebration.

— 16 —
The Name Game

When I met my husband, I wasn't surprised by the fact that he went by his middle name. After all, I have some southern cousins and the boys all go by their middle names too. I knew that was a southern tradition and that was fine.

However, I wasn't prepared when my husband assumed that I would want to use my maiden name as my middle name. "Don't you want to go by Miriam Jones Bradley?" he asked, innocently. Shocked I sputtered a definite no, informing him that I was not going to be a hyphenated woman. That was fine for those who wanted to do it, but not me.

"No, that's not what I mean," he continued patiently. "I mean instead of your middle name. A lot of women do that, retain their maiden name as their new middle name."

I was shocked into silence, which is quite a feat! Give up my middle name? No way! It wasn't going to happen. I informed him that I had waited many years to find someone good enough to give up my last name for, but at no time in my life had I considered that I would be required to give up my middle name. I like my middle name. It is special. I was prepared to sacrifice my maiden name for the right guy, but the middle name? Uh-uh. Wasn't going to happen.

Still a bit perplexed, he shrugged his shoulders. He wasn't trying to change me, just following his tradition, but if that's how I wanted it, he wasn't going to argue.

So, fast forward three-and-a-half years to when I was publishing my Children's Mystery, *The Double Cousins and the Mystery of the Missing Watch*. This book is the culmination of ten years of work. It is a fictional story, but set on my Grandparents' ranch in Nebraska. Many of the daily events in the book really happened to us as kids, just not the mystery. But, when it came to putting my name on the book, something happened.

When I wrote that book I was Miriam Jones. That book was the story born out of experiences on the Jones ranch. My Great-grandpa Jones's picture was going to be used on the cover. I needed to have the name Jones included in my name. Oh, rats.

Don't you hate it when you have to do something you insisted you weren't going to do? The worst part is the moment of admission. "Yes, honey. You were right."

— 17 —

Excited to Vote

I can't wait for November 2nd! It is, after all one of my favorite things in life. On that day I get to go stand in line, receive my ballot, duck into my private little booth — how exciting is that — and have my say.

The thing is, I'm not just looking forward to November 2nd because of the present dissatisfaction with the direction of America. I am excited because this is something that I was raised to deem important. In my family voting was never questioned.

Turning eighteen wasn't a rite of passage in our family because we could move out, but because we could now vote.

I was taught that we vote because we are American; it's as simple as that. After all, it's our right and our responsibility.

The right to vote is an important part of our freedom. It is a gift and we are responsible to take care of that gift. I watched my grandparents and parents get excited about voting. They paid attention to the news. They discussed politics. Then, they made the best decision they could and they voted.

I remember a conversation between Grandpa Jones and my Dad. Grandpa was nearing the end of his life and he was concerned about the direction of the country. He had hoped to leave a better place for his grandchildren. Had he done enough to ensure that? He was born in 1905 and had seen hard times, lived through good government and bad, and had voted a lot.

But he still felt the weight of responsibility. Overheard conversations like that make an impression.

When Ronald Reagan died I sat on my couch and cried while I watched the news coverage. My niece sat with me and watched. I could tell she didn't understand what Aunt Miriam was so sad about. "Ronald Reagan was the first President I ever voted for," I explained. "He was a real American hero."

Even at her young age she understood. Her parents believe in voting too, you see. Now my nieces and nephews, several in their teens, are eagerly awaiting the day they can vote. My oldest niece was devastated to figure out she will miss the 2012 election by less than a month.

It doesn't matter if you are rich, poor, black, white, red, brown, or yellow. You can be unemployed or the CEO of a large corporation. If you are an American and eighteen, you can vote. Why wouldn't you?

It also doesn't matter if you live in South Dakota, South Florida, or South Carolina; on the coast or in the forgotten middle of the country; in Manhattan, New York, or Manhattan, Kansas. Even if you are living in Thailand you can get an absentee ballot and vote.

If you have registered to vote, you just show up at the polling booth and have your say.

If you haven't registered, here's an idea. Why don't you do it on November 2nd ? Then next time there is an election you will be ready and waiting! Just like me.

— 18 —

More Alike Than Different in This Regard

My Dad was drafted into the Army right at the end of the Korean War. As he explained it to me, "I was in basic training and they heard I was coming, so they decided they might as well give up." As any adoring little girl would, I believed my Daddy. Since then, of course, I have learned to watch for the tiny smirk that flickers across his face when he is pulling my leg.

With Veteran's Day coming up I wanted to write about the military because it is a huge part of the culture here in the South. So many young people from this part of the country go off to war.

Of course, there are many theories as to why this happens, such as the opportunity for an education or even just a paycheck. Those reasons certainly hold merit, but I don't think that's all there is to it. I believe there is an underlying desire to do the right thing, a desire to protect the people they love. I believe it involves a basic patriotism that leads to making the ultimate sacrifice, if necessary.

I find myself unable to differentiate between the South and the Great Plains in this column. The statements I have made and the reasons I have given are all very similar to the cultural reasons why so many young people from the Great Plains areas go into the military.

I did a bit of research and I found some striking statistics which not only prove that I am right about the similarities, but also hint at the core of the matter. According to heritage.org, in 2005 the recruit/population ratio in the South Atlantic and the West North Central Regions of the country were nearly equal. The telling part is that the big city areas such as the Mid Atlantic, New England, East North Central (Chicago), and even the Pacific Coast regions were all lower, especially the Northeast regions. The Southern and Great Plains states do send more young people into the military — and it follows — off to War.

Why? This is my opinion, not the result of a complete study of the subject, but I think that people from small towns and rural people — those close to the land — are more likely to stand up for their country. They are more civic minded and recognize more clearly the responsibilities they have to their homes, families, and country. They are also more independent and willing to shoulder their fair share of the load. They don't assume someone else will do it for them.

I've been blessed to live most of my life in such an environment. I'm thankful beyond words to know that Newberry fits into this description because it certainly makes it feel more like home to me. And maybe, just maybe, what my Daddy told me was true. After all, it was when Truman was President and he was a farmer from Missouri. Maybe the enemy heard men from the South and the Great Plains were coming and they signed the armistice. I'm just saying.

— 19 —
Pansies – In the Fall?

The trees are dropping their leaves, and the house across the street is surrounded by the magnificent colors of the season. Just a couple of hours north, our house in North Carolina already went through the change of seasons and I was there to marvel at the beauty of God's creation. Now, here in Newberry I love a good crunch through dead leaves as I take my walk around town. I enjoy the way the light shines through the bright red leaves. I revel in the sight of newly-planted pansies gaily peeking their heads above the mulch . . . wait a minute. Pansies? In November?

I'm sorry, but that's just not right. Where I come from, pansies are definitely Spring flowers. No one in their right mind would plant pansies in the Fall. That would be one colossal waste of time and money. In fact pansies are a definitive sign that Spring has arrived. It took me a second to figure it out, and then I realized our winters down here really are very mild. I bet if the pansies are in a protected spot they would do quite well over the Winter. Amazing. Pansies – a sign that Autumn has arrived. I'm working on it but I'm not quite convinced yet.

I love the fact that here in South Carolina, Autumn does happen, unlike South Florida. Fall is my favorite time of year. I love the loamy smell of the dead leaves, the vibrant colors, and the cool bite to the Autumn air. It is so refreshing after the Summer heat and humidity.

My favorite part about Fall here is the extended length. In South Dakota the trees have dropped their leaves. The colorful season is so short. They have had snow already. The wind has gotten blustery.

In fact the other day they had 65 mile per hour winds, and my brother-in-law had to stay home from work. After all, roofing in winds that strong isn't real smart. So, any spare leaves that were still hanging on are probably over in Minnesota or Wisconsin by now, blown along with the gale force winds of that special storm they endured. The temperatures there are more variable. They can have a day where it struggles to get into the 30's followed by a day near 80 degrees.

I guess, if we aren't going to experience a good snow storm soon, it is best that Fall is extended. Once the leaves drop my brain will be expecting a good snow storm. I'd be happy with three to four inches, just a bit of snow. I'm not holding my breath, though. I know that the big five inch storm we enjoyed last year isn't likely to materialize again anytime soon.

I guess I'll have to watch the weather report and make sure I'm in North Carolina when a storm comes. Then I can enjoy the best of both worlds, an extended autumn—pansies and all—followed by a lovely snow.

I am blessed.

— 20 —

Thanksgiving and Family

The ten years before I got married and moved to Florida I spent in South Dakota watching family grow. During those years my siblings produced ten children. I was the one with the camera. I loved being right there—smack in the middle of family—recording each birth and birthday, every first missing tooth.

In South Florida we had several precious friends, but no family. I was thrilled to move to Newberry because we are only a couple hours from my husband's family in North Carolina and a few hours from my mother's two sisters.

I quickly learned that Newberry is all about family. The hospital is a very family-friendly place to work. If there is a family emergency no one bats an eye if you have to leave. Whenever I took time off to go home to visit, they were all thrilled for me and excited to see my pictures when I returned.

I was a little jealous as I realized that I had landed among people who were enjoying the life I had loved in South Dakota. After all, few people in Newberry had to travel 1500 miles to see their family for Christmas. Their problem was the opposite, how to get visits in to all of the family and not leave anyone out.

My husband's brothers follow their own family tradition, developed about the time my husband left for college. They go hunting. Thanksgiving Dinner to them is a ham sandwich at the cabin in the woods. The women folk are welcome to come, but they are going hunting. My husband and I both know how to hunt, but aren't really interested, so we just stay home or find other people to spend the holiday with.

One year we went to my aunt's house in Georgia. My favorite Thanksgiving, though, was the one that we spent on Edisto Island. It was something I had never done and my sister-in-law — whose husband was, you guessed it, hunting — came and spent the weekend with us. I called my family from the beach and tried to describe it to children who had never seen an ocean. It was kind of surreal.

Since leaving South Dakota I've had to revert to the coping mechanisms I learned growing up. Other than when I was a small baby — which I don't recall — we have never lived in the same town as our grandparents. Many times we lived several hours away, sometimes half-way across the country. If it's not possible to travel, you make new traditions. You have quiet holidays at home. You make family out of friends.

This adds richness to life. Some of our best holidays were those we spent at home. The main problem is how to cook a Thanksgiving Dinner for two. We haven't figured that out yet, so we usually end up with way too many leftovers. This year we might cook our meal and take leftovers to the cabin. Maybe we'll even start a new tradition.

— 21 —

Top Ten for Thanksgiving

Today I did a little more decorating for Thanksgiving. I love Thanksgiving. It is one of my favorite holidays. My husband suggested that I write about all of the things in Newberry that I am thankful for, so here it is.

Miriam's Top Ten Things
to be Thankful for in Newberry

1. My husband. He's at the top of every thankful list.
2. My Church Family. They are a delightful group of loving and caring people who have accepted us unreservedly from the first moment we stepped through the doors of Lighthouse Baptist Church.
3. Our friends and neighbors. We have several really special people that we met here, and they have touched our hearts. They have been a wonderful support through some difficult days.
4. Our house. It has always been my dream to live in a brick home. Now I have a brick home on one of the most beautiful streets in town. I also love that houses are known for the person who built them, or who lived in them for a long time, not for the new owner (that is, we live in "The Johnson House").

5. Good healthcare. The hospital here is surprisingly varied in the services it offers, especially for a town this size. The struggle grows to maintain a "real hospital" in small cities. It should be cherished and supported. In addition, the staff are some of the best I've ever worked with. Since I don't work there anymore I think I can brag without sounding prejudiced about it.
6. Friendly people. People wave to me all of the time. Everyone is interested in hearing my stories and I do like to tell stories. I love that people actually sit on their porches and visit with people who come by.
7. Winter, Spring, Summer, and Fall. I love that we have seasons. I especially like the excitement in the air when it snows, or even threatens to snow.
8. Zesto. I haven't been there in a while but it was one of my first discoveries in Newberry and the retro feel of the place charmed me right off the bat.
9. *Books on Main*. Believe me, this book store is one-in-a-million and we must do our best to buy our books there whenever possible.
10. A walkable town with a vibrant downtown. Not too many cities anymore have a real downtown. I love that you can really find things you need here, and not just at Wal-Mart. I'm thankful there isn't much I need to drive out of town to buy. Every time I walk past the empty storefronts I so desperately want to start a business to fill their emptiness. (Never mind! I am NOT an entrepreneur and have no money for that.)

As I look back over this list the majority have more to do with the people rather than the place. But then, it's the people that make the place, isn't it?

— 22 —

Choose Your Sides

For Thanksgiving my husband's niece offered to bring green bean casserole and macaroni and cheese. I was surprised by the macaroni and cheese. Don't get me wrong; I love macaroni and cheese, but for Thanksgiving? Not a side dish I would have chosen.

Speaking of choosing sides . . . I've noticed a definite difference in the sides offered in restaurants here in the South. You find the above mentioned mac and cheese, grits, sweet potatoes in some form, greens, and of course rice. Oh, and okra; sometimes fried, other times stewed with tomatoes.

In contrast, out west you will find potatoes. Lots of potatoes. They come french fried, baked, mashed — and for breakfast — hashbrowns. You probably will find potato salad. There will be broccoli, green beans, and corn. Maybe some applesauce or peaches with cottage cheese. If there is rice it is usually rice pilaf.

These, of course are also found down here in the South. The difference is more in what's absent out west. No grits, no okra, and if there are greens it's a side salad of lettuce with a little purple cabbage thrown in for color.

I'm not saying we never ate any those things. We definitely ate macaroni and cheese when I was growing up. In fact, after my mother died, we ate macaroni and cheese every other night. It wasn't out of a box either. My sister and I knew how to make that dish and not much else. The other nights we ate pot pies.

Occasionally, my Dad would broil steaks and bake—you guessed it—potatoes.

In our family we also ate rice but not as often as potatoes. We ate sweet potatoes only for holidays. Once my Dad remarried, our new Mom introduced us to spinach and Swiss chard. I had never eaten mustard greens before coming down South. And okra or grits? Not a chance there. I do remember someone gave us a can of okra once. It was slimy and that's all I'm going to say about that.

It's not hard to figure out why there are differences. In past times, cultures depended on the foods they could produce locally. After all, people couldn't afford to ship foods from afar like today. I'm not sure we are better off. Oh, we can find all sorts of non-local foods in the grocery now. That's all well and good, but it comes at a price. The small farms have practically disappeared. Out west big corporations are swallowing up land and the small family farm and ranch is struggling. It is harder for farmers to find local markets for their produce.

The slow food and eat-local movements are a breath of fresh air. I'm certainly not an environmentalist by any measure, but it seems to me the wise use of our resources and promoting locally grown produce is not only good for our local economies, but also for our health. After all, who wouldn't rather eat home grown tomatoes?

— 23 —

George Washington Carver

When I gave the column for last week to my husband for a final edit, he found a couple of holes in my logic. I hate when that happens. By the time I added a few sentences of explanation about sweet potatoes, two things had happened. First, it was too long.

Second, I had a great idea for another column about one of my favorite historic people, George Washington Carver.

George Washington Carver was born to a domestic slave serving an older farm couple in Missouri at the end of the Civil War. She was more of a companion to them and they certainly treated her as family. When slave robbers kidnapped her and her infant son, George, her owner redeemed the sickly baby with his prize horse. The mother was never found. George was raised in this home with his brother, and as a young man went off to school. He eventually earned his Master's degree in Iowa. After graduation he was hired to work at the College in Iowa where he was the first black faculty member.

In 1897 Booker T Washington asked him to work at Tuskegee Institute where he busied himself first with growing crops for the students to eat. He teased them that there were eighteen ways to eat soybeans and he was right. He developed crops that would be profitable but put nutrients back into the soil that had been depleted by cotton. In order to do this he had to develop materials that could be obtained from the crops. He also worked with farmers to develop crop rotation systems to increase soil production.

He was a prolific inventor. He took the peanut, soybean, and sweet potato apart to see what they were made of and then put them together again in different forms. He discovered three hundred things to be made from peanuts alone. Some other inventions were mayonnaise, dyes, shampoos, axle grease, ink, vinegar, soap, and it goes on and on.

Mr. Carver refused to get patents for most of the things he invented. He said that he just went to his lab every morning and asked God what he should discover that day. He believed that God had given him the ideas, so they weren't his to gain from. Now that's a refreshing attitude, isn't it?

President Franklin Roosevelt placed a national monument to honor his accomplishments. He received many other commendations and awards, but he was a humble man who didn't seek recognition. I think the epitaph on his grave says it all:

A life that stood out as a gospel to self-forgetting service.
He could have added fortune to fame, but caring for neither, he found happiness and honor in being helpful to the world.

I love that this man didn't let a rough start in life beat him down. He took the opportunities given him, made more opportunities when he needed them, and used every bit of his knowledge to make a better world for others. I also like that he came from Missouri and Iowa and moved to the South. Now, I can relate to that.

— 24 —

Inch by Inch

My family may never embrace grits, but I believe there may be hope in some other areas. As I write this column I am visiting my family in South Dakota. My sister—who home schools—determined to have her children follow our progress as we drove from South Carolina to South Dakota. "It will help them learn geography," she said. "Besides, it adds to the anticipation of your visit."

So, as we crossed state after state, they would call and ask, "Where are you?" Whenever I approached another major city, I would call them. Sometimes I gave them hints to look up online about things we saw, like major ball team stadiums.

Other times we gave them assignments to look up, like the history of Omaha. Sometimes we called and gave them clues. For instance, "We are just passing Cabela's" at Mitchell, SD, or "Okey-Kadoky" at Kadoka, SD. You have to get creative when crossing South Dakota, especially in the dark, since there isn't a lot out there to look at.

They found great delight in telling me how many inches we had traveled on the map. Let me tell you what, when you are traveling 1680 miles in two days, measuring it inch by inch can be difficult. Especially when you start traveling straight north and they are measuring as the crow flies. We were stuck at "only seven inches to go" for what seemed like hours.

When we left home we made sure we were prepared for a cross country trip during the winter. This is something I learned at a young age. You do not want to get stuck in the middle of a snowstorm on the side of the road and not have chocolate. Oh, and the other essentials like warm blankets, water, candle, matches, and food.

My sister asked if we had plenty of blankets. "Yes," I replied. "Water? Food?." When she was satisfied that I had all I needed she offered a final thought. "That would make an interesting column. I bet they don't have to think about so many emergency items down there."

I told her I was hoping to write a column about some of the things my family has learned about the South since I moved there.

"Well, 'Bless her heart' is in our daily vocabulary now," she said. I laughed.

Yes, indeed. They may never eat grits but they are learning some of the Southern way, inch by inch.

— 25 —

Christmas Traditions

Christmas seems kind of anticlimactic to me this year, since our trip to South Dakota took a bite out of the month. Before we left I decorated the house for Christmas so it would be done when I got home. While there we spent time with two of my siblings and all of my nieces and nephews as well as with my parents. We saw their homes all decorated for Christmas. We gave the children the gifts we had for them. It seemed like Christmas had come and gone.

But it's not over yet. This weekend we get to spend time with my husband's family and I'm excited about that. But how do you get the holiday spirit back? I'm not sure

Maybe it's the weather that's confusing me. There were two fairly cold days when we were in South Dakota but most of the time it was as warm or warmer there than it was here. It snowed . . . everywhere I had been or was going, but never where I was. It's almost like the warm weather followed me out there and back. Interesting.

I've tried playing Christmas music. I've enjoyed lighting the Christmas tree at night and sitting in my living room basking in the glow. I love reading the Christmas cards received from friends all over the country. But somehow, I'm not feeling it this year and our Christmas letter is still unstarted.

Maybe it's because I haven't done any baking yet, but I've about given up on that. With the busyness of the trip and the aftermath, I've decided to postpone Christmas cookies. I think over the next month or so I'll pick a cookie and make one a week. Then I can take them to work and share them there. We sure don't need them here.

But I think I know what will make it right. Our particular Christmas Eve tradition is right here in Newberry. Three years ago my sister and family gave us a freezer ice cream maker. We found a recipe in the booklet for ice cream flavored with candy canes. So now, every Christmas Eve we make peppermint ice cream and while it's getting hard in the freezer we walk down Main Street and enjoy the luminaries. That's a sight I've never seen anywhere before. It's my favorite part of Christmas in Newberry.

But there is the problem of snow. I hear it is supposed to snow in North Carolina for Christmas and it might start Christmas Eve. I plan to be there to experience a White Christmas and I don't want to drive through a snowstorm to get there. So that means we may have to leave earlier than intended. But miss the luminaries? Oh dear, what a choice. But never fear, I have a plan. I'm going to have to take the show on the road and make my own luminaries for the porch there. Maybe it will start a new tradition in that neighborhood. Thanks, Newberry, for another awesome tradition.

— 26 —

Snow on Magnolias

As I left work the other morning, a man rushed through the doorway. "It's cold out there," he said. He shivered in his coat.

"It's a bit chilly", I agreed. "It's winter!"

I've enjoyed this little cold snap. It feels like home. I remember my dismay in South Florida when I walked into the air conditioned mall from the ninety degree heat to see Santa visiting with little children. It just wasn't right.

In addition to the cooler temperatures, the white stuff we enjoyed Christmas was an awesome delight. It surprised me that it had been so long since South Carolina had experienced a White Christmas, but I found myself just as excited as the rest of the general population. Out west it is kind of normal to have a White Christmas, so it really isn't as exciting.

We were in North Carolina where I enjoyed snow all day Christmas. After putting our luminaries out on the porch rail Christmas Eve, we ate peppermint ice cream and waited. Sure enough, the next morning the snow started and didn't stop until Sunday morning. We got nine inches, the most snow I have seen fall in over five years.

It was a winter wonderland. The peace that comes with falling snow is hard to beat. Of course, that is only true if you aren't trying to drive anywhere in it. Otherwise it can be quite frightening and totally frustrating. My husband's brother was unable to come due to the weather, and his daughter who lives around the block did not share my delight at the snow storm.

My heart goes out to all of those people who were trapped in the Northeast with this storm. It's no fun to have plans ruined or be stuck in an airport for days on end. But for some of us, it was a special treat.

Sunday, after the snow stopped we drove down the mountain toward home. The roads were clear and there were no dangerous patches. The view was unbelievably beautiful. I felt like I had somehow traveled to another place. This couldn't be South Carolina. Snow the whole way? No way! But it was true.

When we pulled into Newberry there was still snow on the ground. As we turned onto our street, my eye caught a glimpse of a sight that caused a momentary disconnect. Snow on Magnolias. It sounds like the title of a book, doesn't it? An artsy book.

Anyway, the snow on the magnolia tree was the icing on the cake. I have had my snow. I am a happy camper.

This afternoon we took a walk. It is now fifty degrees here, while back home in South Dakota they are suffering the bone chilling cold of a late December arctic blast and hunkering down to wait out a blizzard. Better them than me.

"Have you had enough snow for a while?" my husband asked.

"Yep," I replied with confidence. "I think I'm good until next winter. Well, unless . . ." I grinned up at him. "A nice 2-5 inch snow this spring would be great, wouldn't it?"

— 27 —

The Power of "Tradition"

For New Year's we ate Hoppin' John, mustard greens, and cornbread. It is our tradition. I remembered the first time I ever heard of this New Year's menu and dug out a piece I wrote in early 2005. I hope you enjoy it.

Sunday I bought black eyed peas. They weren't even on my list, but when I glanced up and saw black eyed peas, I knew. I had to buy them.

It started when I told my boyfriend, Bruce, I was going to visit him in Florida over New Year's. "We'll have to make black-eyed peas and greens on New Year's," he said.

I'm not totally ignorant of Southern culture; most of my mother's family migrated South and all of those cousins are born, raised, and happy-till-they-die Southern. But black eyed peas and greens? Not in my scope of reference. Bruce explained that it was Southern "tradition", and supposed to bring good fortune.

New Year's Day found us tooling around Southern Florida in Bruce's convertible. I saw the Everglades. I was expecting vines, low trees, and lots of slithering snakes and alligators. What I saw was tall prairie grass, like what I imagine the slough in Laura Ingalls Wilder books looked like. We drove clear over to the southwestern coast of Florida before heading back.

Towards evening Bruce said, "We need to stop and get some black eyed peas." Even with his explanation I still failed to realize how strong a tradition it was, so much so that there were none on the shelf. That spot was empty. Next to it was a can of what was called "Hoppin' John", black-eyed peas in a tomato sauce with peppers and jalapenos. We were content with that, but not the lady who stood staring at the emptiness in horror.

"What am I going to do?" she asked, bewildered. "I've been everywhere and there aren't any frozen ones, not even any dried ones. What am I going to do?" she repeated, her voice fading. Bruce suggested the Hoppin' John. She shook her head. "My kids would NEVER eat those." She was now faced with continuing the search, going home empty-handed, or taking the Hoppin' John. She took the Hoppin' John. Oh, the power of tradition.

I enjoyed the meal. The Hoppin' John was spicy, but with Mexican cornbread it was mighty tasty. And I like greens, anytime.

After returning from Florida I went to the grocery store. I was in the vegetable aisle when an employee and customer came toward me. "I looked everywhere and didn't see them," the customer said, in a slight Southern drawl.

"I'm not sure we have any black-eyed peas," the employee said. "But if we do they would be right there." I stopped in my tracks and stared. This being South Dakota, there were none. As the customer walked off, disappointed, I wondered if they might have Hoppin' John, but alas, no. I walked off, strangely disappointed too.

So, when I found them today, I bought some. Now I just need to get greens, make some cornbread, and it can be New Year's all over again.

— 28 —

Winter Wonderland

I feel the need to say right up front, I'm not taking the blame for this storm. Neither am I taking the credit if you enjoyed it. There! I feel better now that I have that off my chest.

I woke up this morning to lots of beautiful snow and three phone messages from my sister. The last one was, "is it a winter wonderland out there?" So, I got on Skype and visited her via the webcam world. I love modern technology! I held my computer up to the window so they could see our snow. She held her webcam up to their window so I could see South Dakota snow.

I am here to announce that my dream has come true. If appearances aren't deceiving, South Dakota and South Carolina are not only side by side in the road atlas, but at least for today they are side by side in real life.

We are snowed in. At least I am not driving into Lexington to work tonight. I called this morning and offered to come in early if there was someplace I could take a nap before the night shift. I explained, "I am quite confident driving on the snow — but the ice that's coming this afternoon, not so much. They decided I wasn't needed enough to merit coming, so I'm staying home. You don't hear me complaining!

I was telling my sister all of this, and she said, "No one can drive on ice." That about covers it. With snow, you just slow down, allow lots of room, and know when to stop (when you can't see the road) and you should be fine. But ice, well, I was never good at ice skating — on foot or in a car.

Last month, on our way back from South Dakota, we followed the ice storm east. Other than a fifty mile stretch around Omaha, Nebraska, we didn't have any ice. However, we saw well over fifty cars in the ditch in a two-hundred mile stretch across Missouri and many were in clumps. Some were upright, some weren't.

"It's a little sobering seeing all of those cars off in the ditch," my husband said. "But as long as we are 'wheels down and headlights forward' we are okay."

It made me even more aware of the differences between winter storms. The truth is that in South Dakota they don't get a lot of ice storms. Generally it is all snow. Sometimes they get freezing rain followed by snow. Then they just stay in because everyone knows you can't drive on ice. Of course, the difference is primarily because it is colder there. For instance, this evening it is minus nineteen degrees. That's a tad nippy! Too cold for freezing rain, certainly.

So, today I sat with my teapot full of gingerbread tea and enjoyed the view out the window. From where I sat — safe and warm — my sister was right. It is a winter wonderland.

— 29 —

Wooly Worms and Weather Men

This past fall my brother-in-law in North Carolina told us it was going to be another hard winter. He knew this because of the wooly worms. My husband commented that the past two years we have been "covered up" in acorns. I was intrigued and started paying attention to the news.

Sure enough, that week the winter weather predictions came out from the national weather people. It seemed that the worms and trees were wrong. Due to *La Nina* we would not have a cold, wet winter. Instead, we would have a cool fall followed by a dryer than normal, warm winter. They even started talking about the drought we might slide back into.

Fast forward four months. If *La Nina* is controlling our weather patterns as they said it would, why, oh why have we had more snow in South Carolina this year than in the past thirteen years all put together?

I'm not a weather-man basher, believe me. I find all of that knowledge and ability intriguing. I depend on the weather people. I'm extremely thankful for radar reports when there is a tornado, a hurricane, or some other potentially disastrous weather on the way.

I love *weather.com*, especially when I need to drive across the country in the winter. I also like to know what the weather will be like when I want to take a walk, when I drive to work . . . you get the picture.

So why do I find myself believing natural creatures more than the weather man, especially for long range forecasting? I believe that people who live close to the earth—those who are in agricultural areas—are more likely to pay attention to the natural world's predictions. After all, the farmers, ranchers, woodsmen, and fishermen all have had to depend on the signs of nature for generations. It's kind of in our blood.

My sister and family live in the Black Hills of South Dakota. My brother-in-law reports that they watch the deer feeding patterns to determine if predictions of major snow storms are true. If the deer are feeding a lot, there will be a big storm.

Just this week, I heard that since the snow was on the ground more than three days, we will have another snow. My husband said the old people say it like this; "if snow stays around, it's just waiting for the next snow."

This folklore is derived from generations of real people observing God's creation. Oh, and that leads me to the main reason I would believe the wooly worms have some validity. They are created by the God of the Universe who gave them everything they need to survive in their environment.

However, he also gave humans the ability to learn and create our weather-predicting devices. While neither way of predicting is fool-proof, they both are helpful. So, I guess you could say we have the best of both worlds. We might as well use it all!

— 30 —

Comfort Foods

Moving to Newberry has proven to be a growing experience and I'm not talking about my character or education. I signed up at work to be on a team for the year-long weight loss challenge. I'm hoping the accountability will help. As far as I'm concerned anything is more fun as a group activity.

Of course I am now thinking a lot about my favorite foods: comfort foods. I think comfort foods are an inherited thing. At least, they are learned. My aunt emailed me after reading my column about macaroni and cheese and she had to comment. She is one of the aunts that moved down South and now has raised a family of Southern children.

She commented on the fact that her kids like mac and cheese for holidays, not something that was a family tradition when she was young. She went on to list her comfort foods: grilled cheese sandwich and tomato soup, chicken noodle soup, macaroni and cheese, and fried chicken, mashed potatoes, and gravy. I had to laugh. She certainly is my mother's sister, for that would be my list too. Well, chocolate and ice cream too, but that goes without saying.

I think it must be something to do with what we were fed when we were young. At work I have a friend from Norway. We were talking about special Christmas traditions and she got quite nostalgic about the homemade ginger ale they made each year for Christmas. By the time she was done talking about it, even I wanted to try it.

One comfort food from the South is cornbread. I love cornbread; it's something we ate, too, but we always put sugar in it. We even like to keep several of those Jiffy Cornbread Mix boxes in the pantry. My brother-in-law from North Carolina calls that "birthday cake".

My Grandma warned me. One time when I was visiting them, Grandma asked me to make cornbread. She showed me the recipe and then she said, "This has sugar but if you ever make it for someone from the South, they don't use sugar."

I think biscuits were more commonly used out west. That reminds me of biscuits and gravy. Sausage gravy. That's something I grew up with. It's also something that isn't on my diet, at least not as much as I would like.

One helpful thing about dieting in the South is the almost year-round availability of fresh fruits. Starting in the early spring we get strawberries, then blueberries, peaches, and finally, apples. We can still get bags of apples up at the fruit stand just this side of Hendersonville.

So, I guess I need to focus on the fresh food, and save the comfort foods for later. I saw this recipe today for blueberry apple pie. If I ignore the fact that it has a pie crust and a cup of sugar, it should fit into my diet, right?

— 31 —

Southernisms 102

When my sister-in-law called the other day she was laughing. There is a Southern gal in their church, a military wife from Atlanta who was bemoaning the fact that her daughter was "fixin' to show out". My sister-in-law was delighted to realize that she knew exactly what her friend meant . . . thanks to me. I had to laugh too.

Actually, the military brings quite a few Southerners to Rapid City because of the Air Force base. About ten years ago, a young man came from the mountains of Tennessee to Rapid City and began attending our church. Soon, he married and brought his young bride.

When winter arrived she came to church and asked around, "Anyone know where I can find a boggan here in town? I looked all over Wal-Mart and even asked, and everyone just looks at me funny."

"A what?" we asked.

"Boggan . . ." she said. "A toe-boggan."

Oh! A toboggan. That we know. We gladly suggested that she try the sporting goods section, next to the sleds.

She was obviously frustrated and replied, "That's what they kept telling me at the store, but I want a toboggan." She reached up and pulled her hands down over her ears. "You know, to wear on your head when it's cold."

Blank stares from the Westerners. "A hat?" we guessed. "A stocking cap.?"

Finally, we understood each other. She wanted a stocking cap, a toboggan . . . of course.

And just the other day I saw another one on Facebook. Our friend from Atlanta posted that she better get some coffee soon or she was just going to fall out.

The first time I heard "fall out" I laughed right out loud. Not because I didn't understand it, but rather because it is so perfectly descriptive that I knew exactly what it meant.

You know, nurses do like helpful shortcuts, especially if it means more time with the patients. When sharing information, acronyms can come in handy. For instance NKA means No Known Allergies, COPD means Chronic Obstructive Pulmonary Disease, CHF stands for Congestive Heart Failure, MI means Myocardial Infarction (Heart Attack) and unofficially — here in the South — just between staff members I have seen DFO . . . Done Fell Out.

I'd love to go to work just for one day in South Dakota and use that acronym. It would be so much fun seeing them try and figure out what I meant. I know, I'm just showing out a bit.

— 32 —

It's All About Respect

As a child I was taught to address adults by their titles, then their names. For example, it always started with Mr., Mrs., Miss, Pastor, Aunt, Uncle, Grandma, or Grandpa. Usually it was their last name that followed the title unless it was an aunt or uncle. It was unheard of to call an adult by their first name. It was a matter of respect.

I'm not an overly proper person. I tend to be kind of informal, but this is one thing that was really ingrained in me as a child, and it stuck with me.

Here's an example. I have really close friends in Wyoming. He is the Pastor of the church I attended while in Nursing School in 1988-1989. He and his wife have become two of my very best friends. I babysat their kids who are now all married with children. He helped perform our wedding. But, despite the closeness of our relationship — he is like the big brother I never had — I call him "Pastor". I just cannot call him by his first name. It might be silly but it is who I am.

Because of this I always get a little uncomfortable when people don't address others properly. A few months ago I overheard a conversation that makes me think I am not alone. I was in an office here in Newberry waiting my turn. An elderly man came into the office and presented himself to the window, chatted with the receptionist, then sat down. He looked at the man next to me and asked, "Did she call you 'darlin'?"

We both looked at him blankly.

"Did she call you darlin' too? She called me darlin'. I'm not her darlin'. I'm not anyone's darlin'." He shook his head. "Darlin'. I wonder if she calls everyone that?"

I chuckled a bit but I knew what he was getting at. It just didn't seem right. Oh, I'm sure she was just trying to put him at ease. It was just her way. She meant no disrespect.

One rule I was taught was to address people with a formal title and let them tell you if they preferred a more informal address.

For the ten years before getting married I was called "Miss Miriam" at church. There were two Mrs. Joneses in the church, so adding a Miss Jones was confusing. In addition, since my nieces and nephews — who all attended there — called me Aunt Miriam, it was easier for the other children to call me Miss Miriam. It was a bit more informal, yet proper.

That title prepared me for life in the South. I feel quite at home with the most used title for women, "Miss". It confused me at first. In my previous life "Miss" meant you weren't married. Here it just means you are a lady. I like it.

While I love being married, it still startles me to be called Mrs. Bradley. I'm thankful that here in the South I can still sometimes be Miss Miriam.

— 33 —

Books, Music, and the Opera House

If you spend any time at all with me you will learn one thing. I hum. Many people believe it means I am a happy person, and I am most of the time. But my humming has nothing to do with my happiness. I hum unless I'm asleep, happy or not. It's a habit born out of a love for music.

If you come to our house and walk into our living room you will know two things about us instantly. We like books and music. We have an L-shaped bookshelf immediately inside our front door, the "Book Nook", and that's really just the beginning of the book collection, believe me!

We have a piano and an antique pump organ. We have shelves and shelves of CDs. And, to combine the two elements, we have a bookshelf full of old hymn books.

Our musical taste leans toward classical and traditional Christian. My husband has some Blue Grass Gospel recordings and I have a couple of Western Cowboy Music CDs.

There are a few other CDs of different types, but basically if it is so loud you can't understand the words, or obnoxious — admittedly our opinion — we don't listen to it.

The South is known for its rich musical heritage. There seems to be no end to the types of music that come out of the South. I have been thrilled to learn that there are several conservative Christian radio stations available here. They just aren't easy to find out west. There's nothing like driving down the road and listening to a good radio station.

The Country Music that is so popular here is also the music of the Great Plains. The agricultural people love their Country Music. One of my strongest memories from visits to my grandparents' ranch in Nebraska was waking up to the smell of coffee and bacon, as well as the sound of the radio playing Patsy Cline or Hank Williams, Jr.

I have been thrilled with the Opera House. We have enjoyed the opportunity to go several times. My favorite events are the classical groups or show tunes.

When Buddy Green came to sing for Pork in the Park, it rained and he had to move into the Opera House. A mutual friend, Rita Ruby, a bluegrass singer from Chicago, was here visiting us and she was able to sing with him. She was thrilled and so were we. We also were able to entice my brother-in-law and his wife down from North Carolina to hear him.

Another memorable event was Doyle Lawson and Quicksilver. I had never heard of him, but Bruce told me he was quite famous and we should take the opportunity to see him in concert. I enjoyed it, but I have to admit it isn't really my type of music. Now if the cowboy singers from the Circle B Ranch outside of Rapid City would come to the Opera House . . . Oh my! I guess it's just further proof I'm not from around here.

— 34 —

Southern Roads

This past weekend I went to a writing conference at North Greenville University. Saturday evening, after two full days, I climbed in my car, turned on and programmed my GPS, and headed for Atlanta as fast as the speed limit would allow. Tired though I was, I remained determined to get in on the last half of a girls weekend with my mother's sisters and their daughters.

My mother was one of four sisters. All of her sisters came south for college. Two married men who made their homes in the South and have lived here most of their lives. Except for me and my siblings, all of the McKnight cousins are VERY Southern. They love teasing me about calling Coke "pop". On the flip side, I have to ask them to repeat things sometimes, because I just can't understand their Tennessee and Georgia accents. Nonetheless, they are my people, and when I'm with them I understand more of why I am the way I am.

All went well until somewhere in Greenville my GPS seemed to lose its brain and told me to turn where there was no street. I was lost. After a panicked call to my husband and the help of a road atlas, I found my way again and was back on track.

As I approached the general area I began to question using the GPS to find my way from the interstate over to Alpahretta where we were meeting. After all, it had already failed me once. It was dark, I was mentally exhausted, and I was alone. Trying to read the MapQuest directions I had printed would have been as stupid as texting while driving — and I'm not that stupid.

So, my great husband got on MapQuest at home and — street by street — talked me in. I arrived frazzled but in one piece. My aunts and cousins listened sympathetically to my ranting about the poorly marked streets, the weird traffic rules, and the traffic in general. They all smiled and nodded. Then my Aunt Rachel offered an explanation.

"You know why the streets change names so frequently here in the South, don't you?" she asked. She proceeded to give a list of five or six names which were all assigned to the same road.

"No, why?" My mind shot to life. This could be a column idea!

"Well," she said. "It goes back to the Civil War. The Southerners changed the names every little bit so the Northerners would get confused and lost."

"Wow! That's amazing," I said. Then my brain blinked. Wait a minute. "Is that true?" I looked at her through narrowed eyes.

She grinned and I rolled my eyes. You see, there's a really good way to tell if my Aunt Rachel is pulling my leg . . . that would be if her mouth is moving, and that cannot be blamed on the South.

— 35 —

Hot and Breezy

I'm sitting on my swing enjoying the record heat — 80-some degrees — and breezy winds. The little spring banner I put out the other day is blowing straight sideways and weather.com says we are having gusts up to 24 mph.

What a beautiful day. I took a walk downtown this afternoon. I've been trying to walk two miles several times a week as part of my weight loss program and for general health benefits. Today, though, I enjoyed the walk more than most times. There were a couple of reasons.

The first was the weather. The air temperature was so warm I actually had to peel off my sweater, and by the time I got home my face was beet red. However, the real reason I so enjoyed the walk was the wind. Whenever I hear the word "windy," or "breezy" in the forecast I get excited. I like windy. I love breezy. It is what I know.

Out west, breezy has an entirely different number than here. Gusts of 24 mph are very common. Breezy would probably be more like 30 mph and windy is 50-60 mph. It's all relative, I guess, but for me, it speaks of home.

Also, when working the night shift and dealing with what I like to call "night shift brain," there's nothing like a walk in a brisk wind to clear the cobwebs away. Today I had that perk, right here in Newberry.

Even though my hair was blowing every which way, I was smiling.

In addition to the weather, I also enjoyed my walk today because it had added purpose. I saved money. Yep, you heard me. I saved money.

Our car tags were due and I had not mailed in the payment, so I needed to make a personal visit to the County Treasurer's Office. I could have driven down to the office, but I decided to make it part of my walk today. After all, have you noticed the price of gas lately? That's a dumb question. Of course you have. It's getting downright ridiculous and it sure makes one think of optional forms of transportation, like feet.

I'm thankful I live in a town where I can still walk to do business, if needed. It's an added blessing.

And now, I think I'm going to have to go inside. The breeziness seems to be increasing. If the weather man is right, we could have some real honest-to-goodness western windiness to contend with tonight. I just hope the trees here can handle it, since they weren't raised fighting the wind the way those western trees were.

— 36 —

Me, a 'Southern Writer'?!?

When I arrived in Newberry I sometimes called myself a writer. Other times I said I was an "author wannabe," but never an author. However, since coming here I have become both. I can confidently say, "I am an author and a writer."

This is the culmination of thirteen years of effort. It is the result of a God-given gift for chatting and sharing stories. It was inspired by my grandparents and encouraged by my family and friends. It was tweaked by my writer's group in South Dakota. My husband — totally believing in my potential authorship — caught the vision of my mystery series and agreed to infuse the project with the needed start-up funds.

All of those were essential but there is an added influence that God chose to use.

The South has a rich history of writers and offers many more opportunities for writers to learn and gather. And Newberry itself has been incredibly supportive and encouraging to my writing career.

Even before my first book came out, Randy at *Books on Main* promised that if it was published, he would sell it. He would also let me have a book signing. Oh, my! Such a dream. When the dream became a reality, he was true to his promise.

In addition, I was offered the opportunity to be on WKDK and Leslie Moses from the *Observer* came calling, asking to do a human-interest article. After my co-worker, Miss Mona, mentioned my book to a friend from one of the local schools, I had a call asking me to come speak on the writing process. This spurred me to develop a PowerPoint presentation that I have enjoyed taking into several schools. Now I am going to Girl Scout troops with the presentation. Such wonderful opportunities. I was amazed and humbled.

Last spring I wanted to start writing a column. Through a series of events which I call "acts of God", I was reconnected with Leslie Moses and she offered the information that the *Observer* was looking for a columnist. I had an idea and they liked it. *Voila!* Here we are. Recently, because of the column I had the opportunity to speak to the AAUW group, prompting the creation of another presentation with its own PowerPoint show.

My writers group in Newberry has helped me fine-tune the beginning of the second book in the mystery series and I have now found it a home with a traditional publisher. Yes, you heard it first, right here.

If all goes as planned, sometime this summer the second Double Cousins Mystery will also be available at *Books On Main*, as well as from many other sources. I am beyond excited.

When people put my book in the Southern Writers section of a bookstore I feel the need to say, "That's not right. I'm not from around here." However, the South has become an integral part of my writing career. Could it be it's not my love of grits that's the most Southern thing about me? Maybe instead it's my writing.

— 37 —

Spring

I feel a little like a traitor to my roots, but I'm delighted to see Spring. Honestly, though, from the comments I'm hearing from the Western front, no one there would fault me. I think they are a bit jealous. They are just holding their collective breath and hoping the sub-zero weather is over and their "snowiest February on record" segues into an early Spring.

Meanwhile, I am reveling in the bursting forth of Spring as evidenced first by the daffodils, which have been waving their bright faces for a couple of weeks, and then by the blossoming trees. The potential for green trees before the end of April amazes me. It really is one of my favorite things about living in the South.

To help it along, I bought a mini spring banner for my front yard. Not a green leaf or tree blossom was in sight, but it was my declaration of readiness.

Yesterday, when I took a walk there was just the hint of a shadow of — could it be? — budding leaves in the very tops of the trees? Now today, they are definitely turning green.

I don't trust it, though. I'm used to the fact that Spring is an on again, off again process. I was talking to my four year old niece today and asked her if she had played outside. "No, it's too cold. Yesterday it was really warm and I played outside, but today is too cold again."

That's Spring in the West. Just a tease of warmth followed by more Winter. After all, March, April, and May are the months that they get the most moisture, and the majority of it comes as snow in March and April.

On the subject of moisture, my husband says calling rain or snow "moisture" is a western thing. I guess it's because there's so little moisture that we count it all. One farmer friend in Wyoming commented on the good crop of wheat he got despite a dry summer, saying, "I got a pretty good crop from two dews and a fog." He was only partly joking.

The risk of an early Spring is that if it gets too warm too soon, all of the buds freeze and you never get to see the pretty lilacs. Those were the only flowering bush or tree I had really experienced. You can imagine my delight the first Spring in Newberry when the dogwoods and azaleas blossomed. The color, the joy, the . . . yellow dusting on my car. What is that yellow stuff? Pollen? You can see the pollen here? Oh my.

I have a niece who is so allergic to pollen, I'm positive she shouldn't visit here in the Spring. I remember one year they came to Georgia for the month of April and she was very sick.

Thankfully, I'm not allergic to any plants so I'll enjoy every bit of our extended Spring, even the yellow dusting on everything. Bring on the pollen, I'm ready for Spring!

— 38 —
Colorful Turns of Phrase

I love those colorful turns of phrase. I've enjoyed learning quite a few new ones since moving here. I try and remember them, integrating them into my vocabulary whenever possible. I love words.

A few weeks ago I spoke to the American Association of University Women here in Newberry, for whom I had put together a presentation using quotes from my grandparents. Afterward, one of the ladies shared an old-timer quote which really tickled my funny bone.

It seems a lady went over to her neighbor's house; her husband was upset about something, so she told her friend, "He can get glad in the same pants he got mad in."

When I decided to write this particular column, I asked my southern cousins to send me some of their favorite sayings. Several of them seemed to be ones I remember from my childhood. I think they may be related more to rural people rather than to where you hail from. For instance, "in a coon's age, over yonder, don't get too big for your britches, and hold your horses." Those are all familiar to me.

However, there were others. One that is definitely reminiscent of my Southern cousins was this one, "Well, shut my mouth!" I can hear them saying it in my head right now! There's also, "I'll be there directly." I would have said it, "I'll be there right away."

My husband has shared some his Mama used. For instance, if someone was frugal — maybe too frugal — she would say, "He's as tight as Dick's hat band." If it was hot outside she'd say, "It's as hot as the hinges on the back gate."

Today I heard one that made me laugh out loud. Someone was talking about a lady who had difficulty with directions and described her as, "so lost she can't find her way in out of a rainstorm". I love it! So descriptive. So colorful.

I know I use phrases that are unfamiliar to most of you. For instance, I say something is spendy if it is expensive. If we get any rain, snow, sleet, dew, fog, or hail, it is called moisture, as in, we sure could use some moisture today. Of course that is from the land where no one carries umbrellas because it doesn't rain often enough or for long enough to need one. The opposite of that was when one of my southern cousins told me it wasn't raining in Chattanooga. The moisture drizzling, misting out of the sky was just "high humidity."

It seems every time my husband's aunt comes over, she says something that just "gets away with me," another new phrase for me. One of my latest favorites, which I've started integrating into my speech, is "I'm all covered up with . . ." whatever it is I'm all covered up with.

There's one more phrase that makes me laugh and that's using the word "slap" for "completely". I'd say more about that, but I only get so many words for this column and I'm slap out.

— 39 —

That Terrible Trash

Maybe it's a symptom of spring fever but the trash along the highway has been annoying me lately. It seems that there is an overabundance, or perhaps I'm just more aware.

Maybe it's because of the huge billboard that catches my eye every time I drive into Columbia. One time, it started a train of thought which so consumed me that I missed my exit. It's the sign with the little girl informing us that litter doesn't cost the government, it costs her! It's a sobering thought. What kind of national debt are we leaving the children? Oh, wait — that's another column.

So, trash and litter have been on my mind. I'm not a neat freak by any stretch of the imagination. I'm fairly organized in my required tasks — being task oriented kind of compels me to be — but I am a "messy". Sometimes the organization is only in my head, so it's a bit strange for me to be annoyed by trash.

Maybe it's the way I was raised. I don't remember my parents throwing anything out the car window that wasn't biodegradable. We were allowed to throw the apple cores out the window — after all, they fed a little creature — but never paper or other garbage. We are supposed to take care of the earth.

My Grandma always paid us a penny for each dandelion we picked in the spring. She said if you get them when they are yellow, they don't spread as fast. This was the same Grandma who informed me that nurses are messy. She said they tended to throw things at the trash cans instead of into them, and if they missed they didn't always pick it up. I was a bit offended and insisted she was wrong, until the next time I was feeling the pressure of too many tasks in too short a time and I threw something at the can . . . Hmmm! Do I hear Grandma laughing?

Often when I'm walking my mind is on something else — maybe my next column — and I don't notice the trash. The other night was the exception. I was walking to a friend's house when a front lawn shouted at me. Yep, you heard me right. There, in front of God and everyone, intruding on the grass of the most impeccably kept yard in Newberry, was a candy wrapper. The lawn shouted, "HELP ME!"

What's a girl to do? I picked up that terrible candy wrapper, carried it to my friend's house, and deposited it in the trash can. Am I becoming my Grandma?

I always give an inner cheer when I see one of those signs which announces who has promised to keep that particular stretch of road free of trash. It's an unappreciated task, for sure.

I was delighted by the article in Wednesday's paper about the wonderful volunteers who spent part of their Saturday picking up litter. The picture looked just like my daydream. You know — the one that made me miss my exit.

— 40 —

Spring is More Than Pretty Flowers

I've often said that Autumn is my favorite season. However, living in the Carolinas is making me rethink that long-held preference. I don't know about you, but I'm loving the beauty and magnificence of God's creation.

Yesterday I drove from Newberry to Hendersonville. Just before the state line I caught my first view of the Blue Ridge. All of the massive color explosion between me and the mountains created a lovely pathway, pulling my car inexorably forward.

The riot of pastels took my breath away. The spring green, yellow, pink, peach, lavender, red, purple, medium green, and the dark green of coniferous trees were overwhelming in their palette. Between the purple of the mountains and the pastels of the trees, it was a sight I won't soon forget.

This is definitely different than Spring out west. First, Spring happens later there. The trees won't really turn green for another few weeks. It is gorgeous there too, but they don't have the abundance and variety of flowering trees, that riot of color. Oh my! I know I'm gushing, but there are just some things worth gushing over.

A second difference is the tendency towards tornadoes. This is something that has kind of shocked me about living in the South. I guess I never paid much attention to the wind storms down here, not until I moved here myself. Now, I know everyone thinks South Dakota and Nebraska get a lot of tornadoes, and they do get some whoppers. But there is a difference.

First, I believe there are more tornadoes down here. I have no statistics to prove this, just my personal experience. I have spent my share of time huddled in a basement under a desk, or under an overpass but I just don't remember them being as frequent.

Secondly, the western tornadoes are most common in the late afternoon or early evening. They are the result of storms coming in from the west. The heat of the day builds the storm clouds and you can see it coming for miles. Because they come from the heat, they are more common in late spring and summer.

Here they sneak up on you when you are sleeping, and that's just scary. The other night I was at work when all of that storminess came, and I was glad I was there instead of at home. There is something comforting about being in the middle of a huge hospital when the wind is blowing. Sometimes you can't even tell there's anything going on out there, although that doesn't completely hold true in a hurricane. Hurricane Wilma in South Florida taught me that.

Of course they don't have hurricanes out west, since there are no oceans in the middle of the country. Their big wet storms with high winds usually come in the winter or early spring, and they call them blizzards.

— 41 —

Gardeners and Farmers

I've been wishing my Grandma Jones was still alive so I could call her and tell her about the garden we're planting in North Carolina. She always had a big garden on the ranch, and even when she moved to town she kept a couple of cherry tomato plants on her porch with a geranium. African violets were her specialty in house plants. That's why I always keep an African violet. She and her sisters loved their flowers and vegetable gardens.

I like planting and watching things grow. I love picking and eating the vegetables. But weeding? Not so much. However, this morning I even enjoyed weeding. I'm sure it won't last.

I feel a strong connection to my family when I'm planting things. It probably stems from the fact that so much of my family — especially my dad's side — are involved in agriculture. We have a lot of ranchers and farmers. And my step-mom was raised on a dairy farm. Even my mother's mom had a garden. It was a rock garden with some cactus, but it was a garden. The other day I saw a cactus at the grocery store and I thought of her. Maybe I need to get a cactus to put beside my African violet.

When I hear of people in the Carolinas farming it causes a "huh, what?" moment. To me farms involve acres and acres of corn, beans, or wheat. I'm talking acres and acres. And ranching, well that involves miles and miles of pastures for the cattle to graze. Oh, my. Now I'm craving Nebraska grown beef-steaks.

It befuddles me a bit to think that here, surrounded by all these trees, could be a farm. But farms there are; farms with all sorts of plants and animals, even fruit farms. Now that's something we didn't have out west. I can't wait to go get some of those Lever Farm strawberries. I am absolutely in love with the broad availability of seasonal fruit here. I'm even hoping to go over to Lexington this spring and pick some blueberries.

We are blessed to live in a nation with good land and many natural resources. I'm convinced we need to eat the things we can buy locally and in season. After all, then we don't have to pay for all the fuel to get it here. Everyone I know prefers fruit and vegetables straight off the tree or vine, rather than that which has been picked in California, Mexico, Chile, or Peru, and shipped here. It also helps all of those small farmers, and in my book, that's the best deal of all.

Our gardening friends from work and church are listening with interest to our stories of gardening. They're more impressed with this year's plans. The last few years we have tried growing upside down tomatoes in Newberry without much success. Mr. Jimmie says we just confused the poor plants. After all, would we grow if we were hung upside down?

— 42 —

Whose Garden Is This, Anyway?

This morning after doing some revisions on my book, I headed out to the garden for a little weeding and planting of marigolds. It has come to my attention that by planting the beautiful flowers I so enjoy in my vegetable garden, I can help keep the bad bugs away. What a deal! So out I went with my trowel and two flats of marigolds.

I marched down the edge of the garden thinking artistic thoughts about the blank slate we have in this 40 by 100 foot plot of dirt. I envision it filled with plants and flowers. I want it that way right now, but I know it will take several years to get there. As I walked and thought, I started creating a column in my head. It would be so good.

I set my flats down by the 4 by 40 foot bed that holds our "kitchen garden" and pulled a few ragweeds. I stood up and turned around, remembering I would need my gardening gloves from the house.

In a single instant my beautiful, artistic, peaceful, creative moment was completely shattered. There in the middle of the path I had just traversed sat a SNAKE. A very big, very BLACK snake.

I screamed.

Now, I knew this snake was around. I had been introduced to it a day or two before by my husband and his nephew. When I expressed my dismay, I had been informed that this was a good snake. A friend. Yeah, right.

"No, really. It kills mice."

Oh. Well.

So as my heart beat at least 200 times a minute I reminded myself of these facts. This snake is my friend. My friend. That was NOT working. It kills mice. I stomped up to the house where I informed my husband that if that snake and I were going to cohabit the garden, he needed to have a conversation with the snake and explain it needed to kill the mice quietly and stay out of sight.

He laughed at me. Then he went with me to the garden where the snake was slithering across the warm dirt from one side to the other. My husband explained that not only do black snakes kill mice, they keep bad snakes away. In fact, when we looked online we found that, according to the Davidson College Herpetology Lab, they eat a variety of animals, including small rodents, lizards, frogs, insects, and other snakes.

I sighed. I could see I was not winning this one. "I get it," I assured my husband, "but this will require retraining my brain." The snake I remember hearing about was the prairie rattlesnake and they are bad. I have even taken care of people in the ICU who were bitten by one. And the way my brain works — if one snake is bad . . . they all are.

So, we have a garden in North Carolina — a garden with vegetables, marigolds, and a snake who is my friend. Great. That's just great.

— 43 —

Of Cows and Contentment, An Ode to Beef

On my way back into town Saturday morning from Lever Farms I saw a sight that made me smile. Cows. Yep, right there by the road in a beautiful pasture, fifteen or twenty head of Black Angus cattle grazed, contentedly chewing their cud. I felt the corners of my mouth lift right along with my spirit. I wondered to myself, why on earth do those cows make me so happy?

I'm pretty sure seeing a pond of fish wouldn't have had the same effect.

It isn't hard to figure out, really. If you follow this column you know that my dad's people are ranch folks in Nebraska. If you've read my children's mystery you know that I spent quite a bit of time on a ranch as a child. And, face it, ranches are about cattle. In cow country, if you go anywhere near a feed lot, or are even down-wind from a feed lot, you will experience what locals call, "the smell of money." My husband likes to call it "essence of cow", or *eau de bovine*.

Besides the obvious childhood connections, I think I like cows because they are such useful animals. After all, so many of my favorite foods come from cows. There is the obvious beef. My husband still insists that if it didn't moo, I don't think it's meat. That's not quite true but close enough.

A second and possibly more important reason is that I love all of the products that come from milk. I love milk itself. I love yogurt, sour cream, and butter. I love cream in my coffee. Cheese is good any time of the day. And, as far as I'm concerned, ice cream is the world's most nearly perfect food. I actually believe I could live on ice cream, especially chocolate. But chocolate is a different topic altogether.

There is a big push now for healthy low-fat milk products. I'm not too sure about that. My Grandpa Jones lived to be almost 93 and for most of his life he drank raw milk, straight from the cow. When he was eighty they retired and moved to town. He grouched about the fact that he couldn't get "the real stuff" and the milk they bought at the store just didn't cut it. In fact, for his cereal he bought half-and-half because it tasted more like "real milk."

Yesterday I saw a bumper sticker in Newberry. I couldn't quite read the last word, but I believe it said "Eat Beef – The West Wasn't Won With Salad." That made me laugh. I like salad, but there is no way, no how it compares to a good pot roast. It can't even compare to good ground beef.

Anyway, that is about all I have to say on the topic. No, there isn't any deep philosophical comment. I just like beef. So, I guess you could call this my Ode to Beef.

— 44 —

The Niece Speaks

One thing I appreciate about the South is the importance of family. I am going to take advantage of that this week and share a blog entry my fourteen-year-old niece posted at http://justwhatithink-joyful.blogspot.com

She is a writer and I am so proud of her. She shared so eloquently one trait of South Dakotans I thought you would enjoy. So, with her permission, here is a piece from Mandy.

I already did a story on Homeschoolers so it's only fair I do a story on South Dakotans. We are, to put it quite simply, masters at understating the obvious. Then again, in different circumstances we are masters of overstating things.

I'm not sure why we can't just say things like they are but I think it started back at the Black Hills gold rush. The first people out here said, "The winters are a bit difficult." Yeah, right. About half of you died. And they also said, "There is a ton of gold!" No. There wasn't a lot of gold. So, I figure it's just in our nature.

We like the word "breezy". If you ever hear a South Dakotan say that word, assume they are lying because it's not breezy. "Oh, look — the wind just blew that car over!"

"Yeah, it's a bit breezy." That's us!

Last winter, we went to the grocery store. Most people would take the hint that it's too cold to drive sixteen miles into town when it's

thirty degrees below zero, but our family is home schooled.
Stubbornness issues again. Sigh.

We drove into town anyway. We got our stuff and went to the check
out aisle and the lady says, "A bit nippy today."

"Sure is," Mom replies.

Down-playing and over-stating are just always going to be part of
South Dakota, I'm afraid. But then again, if we were normal there
wouldn't be anything special about us. We are, after all, the selected
guardians of our national monument, Mount Rushmore. I mean, just
think about it, George Washington's head is 60 feet tall!

There is just one more thing I wish to say about South Dakotans.
We are also stubborn and I hope we always stay that way. One example
of this is when a man rode on his bike all the way from South Dakota to
Washington D.C. to be at a rally for blacks' civil rights back on April
28, 1963. Stubbornness issues? You betcha!

Miriam here again . . .

When I read this piece the similarity to the South struck me.
Southerners are also very good at overstating and understating.
Why? I believe hard times lead us to utilize the tools of
hyperbole and humor. Why whine about the weather? It won't
do any good. However, maybe minimizing the pain will help.
Besides, humor is always a good thing, isn't it?

Thank you for indulging this proud aunt! I think my nieces
and nephews are the most amazing kids in the world . . . and
that's an understatement!

— 45 —

The Weeds of Our Lives

I'm pretty sure weeds grow faster here in the South. I guess it has to do with the fact that we get more rain than the Great Plains, which, after all, were originally called "The Great American Desert". They depend on a spring snowstorm to start the growing season. Then, often the last part of May and the first week of June is pretty wet. However, by the Fourth of July it can be really dry and all of the grass on the prairie is brown.

Out there you don't have a garden unless you water. That definitely is not the case here. We were away from our garden in North Carolina for one week and when we returned, the ragweed had nearly choked out our little plants. I couldn't believe my eyes.

So I've taken to going out in the morning when it's cool and the ground is still moist from the dew. The weeds are easier to pull and the mosquitoes are less thick. Besides I find it a relaxing peaceful activity. It gives me a sense of accomplishment to set the rows right again and rescue those little plants from death by crowding.

I've learned that I have to be persistent. If I let my guard down and neglect the garden for even a couple of weeks, it will be hopeless. So, I do my best to weed a little each day I'm here. Then, I hope, it won't be too much at once.

It pays to stay on top of it. I was out again this morning undoing the damage of a few days away from the garden. It didn't take as long this time to set it right. You see, if you keep at it and can get the roots out with the weed, they don't come back as thick.

Everyone tells me I need to mulch. I've started thinking they might be right. That way I'll have even less weeding and maybe I'll actually have time to sit on my new deck and watch my garden grow. But, for now, I weed.

The other morning I spent over three hours pulling ragweed. You can do a lot of thinking in three hours. One thing I thought about was the similarity between pulling weeds and training children to do right in the midst of the world we live in.

Like the plants, they need protection from the "weeds" in this world that would like to take up all their space and choke out their ability to develop into the people they could and should be. It's up to us to pull those "weeds" and protect them until they are big enough to shade out the weeds themselves. They need the "mulch" of good friends and positive influences in their lives while they are little. We hope as they grow older they will pull out their own "weeds".

I just wish I could get my plants to pull the weeds that want to choke them. But, then again, I would lose some great thinking time, wouldn't I?

— 46 —

Honor the Fallen—Peacefully

We need to buy a new flag for our little banner holder in the front yard. Last year's flag is getting pretty worn and I won't put it out in that shape. I've had a spring banner hanging for the past few months but with Memorial Day coming up 1 want an American flag.

We bought one the other day for our place in North Carolina. I like having an American Flag in front of my house. It says something, something I am very proud to say. I love my country.

I was pleased to see an article in the paper about the ROTC and their annual flag retirement ceremony. I don't think a lot of people really know what to do with worn out flags. It makes me sad to see a torn flag flapping in the wind.

I'm thankful that I was raised in a flag-waving patriotic family. I'm thankful now to live in a state where we are proud of our country and take offense at those who would besmirch the character of our soldiers.

We were downtown a few weeks ago visiting with the receptionist while we waited for an appointment We got on the topic of the Westboro Baptist group from Kansas. I have to say right now that they are an embarrassment to the name Baptist, and to the state of Kansas. I am a life-long Baptist and I have strong family ties in Kansas and I can tell you that they are not at all popular with Baptists or folks from Kansas. It makes me sick that they are doing all of this in the name of God. All I can say is God is the righteous Judge and He will take care of it someday.

A friend in Newberry made this comment, "Those folks just need to come down here and meet a few Bubbas. They'd set 'em straight."

Evidently, the Bubbas in Brandon, Mississippi, did just that back in April. Apparently, the townsfolk of Brandon determined that the funeral of their soldier would not be disturbed, so, well, let's just call them "roadblocks" were put in place (parking behind any vehicle with Kansas plates) so none of the Westboro group could make it. There was no protest at that funeral.

In my book, we need more of that kind of response. Normal people standing up and saying, "No you won't. Not in our town. Not today."

I'm thankful that those soldiers were willing to make the ultimate sacrifice so that I can live in peace and safety. They need to be honored and their families need to be protected from the additional grief caused by these "wackadoodles."

So, if you hear of any of them coming to our town, call me. I'll take my car over to their hotel, park behind them to block them in, and find somewhere else to be until the funeral is over. I'd do it in a heartbeat! I may not be from here but I sure could act like it for a bit!

— 47 —

Gettin' Beachy

In the *Newberry Magazine* the other day I saw an advertisement for *Books on Main* and it caught my eye – a photo of a beach chair and some books. The point was that you need to get the books you will want to read when you go to the beach.

The whole idea of beach vacations was foreign to me when I moved here. I enjoyed going to the beach in Florida — It was only twenty minutes from our house — but that was just to walk on the Hollywood Broadwalk and have breakfast at one of the open air cafes. I loved that. It calmed me and I could look straight out at the ocean and see nothing human. That was quite a lifesaver for a South Dakota girl plunked down in teeming, crowded South Florida.

Anyway, when we moved to Newberry, I began to realize that "going to the beach" was something of a tradition. It was THE place to go for a week, or even for a long weekend. I couldn't wrap my mind around it. What would you do there? I don't enjoy sitting in the sun getting all sweaty. I don't enjoy being surrounded by hundreds of people showing off more skin than is attractive. That is just not my scene.

So I listened and thought about what we do back home, and I realized that it isn't so different. We go to the lake, the creek, or the river. Basically, we find the closest nice body of water and we go sit beside it and read books, visit, play in the water, and make

S'mores at a campfire. That's not so different, I guess, except if we eat fish, it's a trout fry, not a crab boil.

I finally discovered the reason people within driving distance of the ocean have to go. When we finally sold the house in Florida we decided to go to the beach for Thanksgiving to celebrate. We went down to Edisto Island and rented a house.

It was magical.

I spent every possible moment roaming the mostly empty beach, picking up seashells, watching the waves come and go, and worshipping God. The awesomeness of Creation is just impossible to avoid at the beach. It was a trip I will never forget. I stood on the sand barefooted and called my family back in South Dakota.

We haven't had a chance since then to go back, but the other day I had to laugh at myself. I told my husband, "I need to see the ocean. I need to go to The Beach." Maybe there is hope for me yet. If I don't have Southern roots, maybe I'm at least putting out tendrils.

So, next beach trip you make, stop by *Books on Main* for your reading material. I know of a great mystery for the young reader: my first book, The Double Cousins and the Mystery of the Missing Watch is there now, and the second will be out in July. Maybe you could get it for your late summer trip!

— 48 —
Thankful

Every time I drive toward the mountains, I feel like I'm going home.

It started early in our marriage when we were frequently driving to North Carolina to take care of the house we inherited. As we approached the mountains, I felt the tension and stress from living in South Florida slide away.

I guess it reminds me of the Black Hills of South Dakota. The moment I first see the Blue Ridge reminds me of that moment when the Black Hills come into sight on I-90 between Wall and Rapid City, SD, and I know I'm almost home. Besides, it is my husband's family home and to me family is family, whether it's his or mine. I'm all about the people and the relationships.

I am repeatedly amused by the inevitable question when people find out we have a house near Hendersonville, "You have a house in the mountains?" Disbelief and a tinge of jealousy show in their eyes.

I smile, shake my head, and try to explain. "Yes, but it's not like that. It's a lot of work." We are in the process of cleaning out and fixing up my husband's childhood home. In fact, when people gush about all of the wonderful things to do in the Hendersonville area, I am pretty clueless. We don't have time to enjoy many of those things.

I'm not personally familiar with having a summer house to flee to when it gets hot, although my husband has pointed out many houses in the neighborhood that were "summer houses" when he was a kid. One belonged to three unmarried sisters who were teachers in Miami and spent every summer in North Carolina. Now it belongs to Bruce's brother.

As a child, my circle of acquaintances was either involved in church ministry or agriculture. I don't know any Pastors who take off for the summer. As for agriculture, farmers and ranchers do not get away from home for any extended period of time. A short weekend or overnight trip is a luxury. Someone has to care for the animals every day, sometimes twice a day.

Even though it isn't in my realm of experience, this week I can certainly relate, since the weather has provided an understanding of the motivation for fleeing to the mountains. As you know, I don't enjoy this heat and humidity. I find myself wishing I could retreat to North Carolina and stay there, work or not. The thing is that it has been warm there too. Sure, it's the usual five to ten degrees cooler, but with the humidity, that's still warm. Besides the house there doesn't have central air conditioning.

So, I guess I'll be happy where I need to be for the day. If it's in Newberry, I'm thankful for my central air conditioner. If I get to head north, I'm thankful for the cool night air and those five to ten degrees. A person sometimes just has to decide to be thankful no matter the situation, doesn't she?

— 49 —

Okra, Oh My!

Why I planted an entire forty foot row of okra is beyond me. I have no idea.

It's not that I hate okra. I can't say I'm really impressed by it, but I wouldn't say I actively dislike it. I just don't think I like it enough to plant forty feet of it. But, plant it I did! After all, the package was open and I didn't want to waste any seeds.

Okra is not something I ate back home. The first time I experienced okra was in California during my teenage years. When we moved there, the church had a welcoming food shower and one of the items we received was a can of okra. A store bought can.

Why someone gave us okra I don't know. Maybe they were geographically challenged and thought that since we were from Nebraska we were from the South and would like it. I'm just guessing, but I can't think of a better reason.

Let's just say that I will never eat store-bought okra again. Slimy stuff.

Some fifteen years later I was in Georgia visiting my Grandparents who had moved there from Colorado to be close to two of their daughters. Grandpa and I were invited to friends for dinner and he asked me if I had eaten fried okra. He explained that while he had no use for any other kind of okra, fresh fried okra was "pretty good stuff, Susie." He said I should give it a chance.

I did, and he was right. It was really quite tasty!

Since coming to Newberry I have been introduced to okra and tomatoes which is edible, even pleasantly tasty, but not something I would choose to eat every day. My husband likes it. He also tells me that his mother used to take okra, corn, and tomatoes and can them together. She called it soup mix and it was the base for many of the soups he ate as a child. He also tells me that his favorite summer meal was fried okra, creamed corn, and fresh sliced tomatoes — the tomatoes preferably still warm from the sun.

So, when we were planning a garden we decided to have some okra. I thought it would be fun to try it different ways, and I thought it would be great to have some soup mix like his Mama used to make. We're not sure we can, but we want to try and recreate his Mama's fried okra, too. I'm sentimental that way, I guess.

But a forty foot row? That's kind of unexplainable. Of course I have no idea what an okra plant looks like, how much it produces, or any other pertinent facts. So, if we are drowning in okra in a few weeks I guess I'll just chalk it up to ignorance and share.

Okra isn't like zucchini is it? You know . . . when you have to put a bag of zucchini in everyone's car at church when they aren't looking?

— 50 —
The Problem With Bambi

The other night I glanced out the back door and there, in the middle of our North Carolina garden, was a beautiful deer. It startled me because my husband has said many times that they have never seen deer in this neighborhood.

I hollered for Bruce to come take a look which, of course, startled the deer and they — yes, there were four of them — ran off into the neighbor's underbrush.

Great, I thought. Now we have to worry about the deer eating our garden.

I am very familiar with the effects of deer on greenery.

In Rapid City, SD, they have had quite a problem the past fifteen years. The city sits in the middle of the Black Hills and Rapid Creek runs right through town. When it gets dry and hard to find food up in the hills, the deer come into town and wreak havoc on the gardens and plants.

Some people think they are "pretty" and put feed out, which makes other people angry because they can't grow anything but marigolds. Not to say anything bad about marigolds — I love them — but it's nice to have variety in what you can put around your yard.

So, the city fathers instituted a policy of letting certain trained hunters shoot the deer in town to keep the population under control. In addition, the average person has instituted various individual measures to protect their gardens and plants. My parents fence their garden.

Our garden is a hundred by forty feet so fencing it would be no small project. I was looking for a different solution, preferably one less time consuming and less expensive. Some friends and family suggested sitting on the deck and shooting them, but that is neither legal nor safe. And while I do like venison, I prefer the western sort. The deer here eat a lot of acorns and the meat is much stronger.

So I began to ask and research. Several people, including a friend in Newberry, suggested getting hair from the beauty shop to put around the garden. That evidently has worked quite well for many folks.

I also was told to hang Irish Spring™ soap around the garden, sprinkle the plants with pepper, and even string old VCR tape around the garden like a fence. Evidently, if you pull it tight, it buzzes in the wind, and the sound is annoying to the deer. Unfortunately the thought of stringing all of that VCR tape was annoying to me.

So far, since they haven't done anything but check out what was available at the "Deer Salad Bar" over at the Bradley Place, all I've done is sprinkle a bit of pepper. I think we might try the soap method. I'm not sure we can get enough hair to sprinkle clear around the garden.

I'm hoping the lush green terrain offers them enough options that they won't want to deal with our little garden. And, just in case, I planted more vegetables this morning. I'm afraid I'm addicted to planting. But that's another column, I think.

— 51 —
Locally Grown—Food, That Is

It's strange how those tasks that seemed created to torture us as children are now a lot more enjoyable, almost fun!

Friends from church gave us cucumbers last Sunday, and in exchange we gave them a couple of watermelon radishes we experimented with this year. Tomorrow we will feast on new red potatoes, Swiss chard, radishes, lettuce, peas, and squash from our garden. To say we are enjoying the garden is an understatement.

I was excited this past weekend to see that the farmer's market had opened again for the summer here in Newberry. It seems "locally grown" is taking off.

According to the Appalachian Sustainable Agriculture Project report from 2007, consumer focus is shifting from organic to locally grown. The report says that if just half of the families in Western North Carolina spent eleven dollars a week on locally grown food during the four month growing season, $36.5 million dollars would stay in the local economy. What a boon that would be for the small farmers.

The ASAP report also indicated that people will choose locally grown if it is comparably priced. The South Carolina Department of Agriculture website states the same thing and even has a nice chart showing which crops are available in which months. I was amazed that there are so many fresh vegetables here year round. You can also find a listing of places where you can buy locally grown products.

It seems that more and more people are growing their own gardens. The Associate in the garden shop at Wal-Mart in Hendersonville told us it's the busiest year he's ever seen. Two of my co-workers are gardening for the first time this year. The sense seems to be that we need to learn or relearn these skills, since we may need them again.

I'm thankful that I'm from agricultural people. We were town folk, but since my parents were raised on the farm/ranch, they enjoyed having a garden whenever they could. It just goes to prove that you can take the kid off the farm, but you can't take the farm out of the kid.

They passed some gardening knowledge on to me. For instance, my mom taught me the most effective way to use a hoe. I really need to call and thank her for that lesson. My husband also grew up helping (reluctantly) in the garden, so between us we know the basics. What we don't know we can ask or find online or in a book. It's funny, but we seem to have a lot more interest in gardening than we did when we were kids.

So, if your kids are bored this summer, why not take them to a farmer's market to get some fresh produce? Better yet, why not torture — I mean teach — them about gardening? They might like it now, they might not. But, they will know where food comes from, and how to get it for themselves. They might even thank you for it . . . someday!

— 52 —

Independent? United?

Everywhere I look there are reminders that the 4th of July is next week,. When I walked downtown this morning, they were putting out the flags on Main Street. Even the blooming crepe myrtles coordinate with the flags and banners.

Words like "independence" and "united" run through my head. While I still believe we live in the best country in the world, I wonder sometimes if those words are really still true in America.

We are constantly bombarded with fighting between our elected leaders and reminded of our differences by people who speak about the red states versus the blue states. I don't feel very united.

And, with all of us so dependent on the government to provide many of our daily needs as well as foreign governments to lend us money, I really question our independence.

This week I was reminded of what America is all about, how it is supposed to be. I have a friend who moved from South Dakota to Minot, North Dakota. We still keep in touch via Facebook. I have watched in horror as the flooding threatened and then consumed, not just her home, but her entire neighborhood, indeed an entire section of her city.

As I watched the reports something struck me. These people didn't holler for the government to come save them. No, they loaded their belongings into cars, vans, trucks, and cattle trailers and emptied out their houses. Those whose homes weren't threatened showed up to help. People who had space took in families, belongings, or both. Once the evacuees' belongings were safe, they went back to help someone who wasn't done yet. People lent their RV's to perfect strangers and even stocked them with food. They were united against the force of nature that threatened their community.

The thing is, the people in North Dakota are a proudly independent, pull-yourself-up-by-your-bootstraps sort. They don't ask for help. They believe in doing it themselves. But, when they come to the end of the rope, they will call out for help. And, if you are one of the lucky ones who isn't experiencing the trial, you get under the rope, ready to catch.

That's independence and united rolled into one situation.

Thankfully, in the time I've been in Newberry, we haven't had any major disasters. I get the sense, though, that people here would be the help-each-other-out sort. This town is full of people who get real joy from helping others and I am privileged to know several of them.

I believe this is a city-country difference. People in the small towns and rural areas are more in touch with their neighbors, feel more connected. When a disaster strikes, they help because they know these people and they know it could just as easily have been them.

I pray that we won't ever have to find out how well we work together in the face of disaster, but if we do, I'm thankful Newberry is a place filled with people ready to stand under the end of the rope.

— 53 —

Amber Waves of Blueberries

We saw what looked like a wheat field the other day. I was pretty sure it wasn't, because I think of wheat as a western crop. But then I saw the article in the paper about the bumper wheat crop this year and I realized there is still so much I have to learn about the plant life down here.

I think of wheat fields as vast, reaching clear to the horizon. I have friends in Wyoming that grow wheat and I've ridden the combine. It's an experience, believe me. But, wheat? Here?

Oh well. I'll catch on eventually.

I've also been pleasantly surprised by the crepe myrtles this year. I was walking the other day and talking to my husband on the phone. I described the trees to him and asked him what they were. He told me he would have to see them. So, I took a picture on my phone and sent it to him. "Crepe myrtles," he said.

Was I blind the last three summers? I don't remember them being this impressive. Maybe it's just a good year for crepe myrtles too! I wish I could take one home to Mom for her birthday, but it would never survive the South Dakota winter.

Yesterday I went to a blueberry farm after work and picked seven pounds. I've picked chokecherries, mulberries, and wild grapes, but never blueberries. It was so cool and peaceful in the middle of all of those beautiful bushes, and they were simply covered up in dark purple berries.

Today we had to tie up some of our tomato plants. The biggest one, a cherry tomato plant, is six feet tall. I told my parents this on the phone and I could hear the amazement in their voices. Six feet tall? Incredible. I remember watering and watering tomato plants in South Dakota and being pleased when they reached three or four feet tall. Not here in North Carolina. God waters them here. I told my husband it reminds me of the story of Jack and the Beanstalk. I almost expect to look out in the morning and find it has grown up to the sky!

We've also been enjoying watermelon this summer. I've purchased it various places, but as long as we thump it, we get a ripe one. I took some to work the other night, and they were asking where I had purchased it because it was so sweet. I told them, but reminded them to be sure and thump them to get the best results. They didn't know how to thump watermelons. Do you?

The idea is that you bend over putting your ear close to the watermelon and thump it with your finger. You pick the watermelon with the lowest tone. I learned this as a child and it works almost every time.

I would tell you a story about thumping watermelons, but I've reached my five-hundred words and besides, I need to go make a blueberry ice cream pie!

— 54 —

Beautiful Bricks

As a child, I dreamed of living in a brick home. It started when we came out to Athens, Georgia, one summer to visit family. When I saw my Aunt's house I fell in love. I thought it was the safest house I had ever seen. Surely brick would never burn down. Right then and there I determined that I would one day live in a brick home.

There aren't many brick homes out west because the materials aren't as readily available. The soil is mostly sandy, not clay. There are some stone houses, especially near stone quarries, but most are wood homes. My Dad was actually born in a sod house in the Sandhills of Nebraska during the Depression, because that was the only material my grandparents could afford at the time. They were that poor. And then they went completely broke and had to give up their property, including the sod house! Can you imagine?

But I digress.

When we were looking for a house in Newberry I was delighted at all of the brick homes. We looked at some of all types — except sod — but I was excited when the house we decided to buy was brick. My dream had come true at last.

I love living in a brick home, but I enjoy looking at architecture of all kinds. Nothing makes me crazier than driving through a neighborhood where every house is exactly the same.

Why have today's architects thrown creativity and variety out the window? I just don't get it.

I'm thankful that Newberry isn't one of those places. We have neighborhoods where every house is different. Oh, I know the mill villages tended to have homes that were all the same, but as time passed they took on individuality through renovations and paint.

I get such pleasure from walking around town looking at all of the houses. We have stopped in front of a house to admire and comment more than once, only to realize that the owner is sitting on the porch listening to us. Don't be surprised if you see us commenting on your house's architecture some day.

Downtown Newberry is a veritable feast for the eyes of the architecture lover. My favorite building is the Bergen building with its design, reminiscent of Native American art. I love standing beside the City Municipal Building on Main Street. Gazing at the building with the brick street in its foreground I can almost imagine myself in Broken Bow, Nebraska. They have a few brick buildings in their downtown, and a brick street. Of course, with a name like Broken Bow, they have some Native American designs in the brickwork.

But a few years ago there was a fire in downtown Broken Bow and almost an entire block of businesses burned. It was a sad sight, all of that empty space. They were brick buildings, too, which I guess proves my childhood belief incorrect. I'm a bit stubborn though, you know. I still love brick.

— 55 —

Cowboys in the Park

It's not like I was hurting for something to do last Friday. I had a huge list of tasks that needed accomplished and a class for work on Saturday, so I really needed to stay home and put my nose to the grindstone.

However, once I saw the notice in the paper that the concert in the park downtown was Cowboy Music, I knew there was nothing on the list that couldn't wait — or wouldn't have to.

When I got to the park I couldn't believe my eyes. There were cowboy hats in the town square. Cowboy hats on people wearing jeans and cowboy boots. I could feel my heart rate jump. I picked a park bench close to the microphones. I wanted to hear every word.

Oh my. For the next hour I sat and alternately resisted the urge to jump up and twirl across the grass like a child unable to contain her joy, or sit and wail because I missed my family, especially my Grandpa Jones.

They sang a lot of the old cowboy songs and the crowd sang along. I heard comments about memories from the picture show when they were children. My memories were a bit different.

I remembered helping Grandpa saddle Brownie, the horse he kept for the grandkids to ride. I remembered riding with Grandpa to get some cows in and having my glasses knocked off my face when I failed to see a branch. I remembered watching hours of the old westerns on TV on Sunday afternoons at

Grandpa and Grandma's ranch. They all paraded through my head.

When they sang a song by "Grandpa Jones" from the *Hee Haw* TV show I laughed because my Grandpa Jones loved watching that show. When they sang a song asking where the cowboys have gone I wanted to stand up and shout, "THEY ARE STILL THERE!"

I thought of my cousin Gordon, riding across the Sandhills of Nebraska on his horse as he works his ranch. I wished every one of those people there could see a real cowboy, on a real ranch. I felt like I knew something they didn't know. I felt blessed.

It was cool—one of those two nice days—and there was a chilly breeze. If I closed my eyes I could imagine myself in Nebraska or South Dakota. By the middle of the concert I was shivering but I certainly wasn't going to get up and go anywhere.

I was right where I wanted to be, enjoying an evening in Nebraska and South Dakota right here in downtown Newberry, South Carolina!

Speaking of downtown, Newberry's downtown is a treasure which should be nurtured. I've been glad to hear of the cooperation in town among the college, the hospital, the downtown merchants, and other companies. I hope that means even better days for our city. I'm excited for July 30th and the hospital foundation rummage sale and downtown merchants sidewalk sale. I'll be at Books On Main during their business hours signing my new, just released book, *The Double Cousins and the Mystery of the Torn Map*! Come by and say hello!

— 56 —

Fresh Out of Ideas

I was looking through the computer file of columns I have written for the Newberry Observer. There are a lot, over fifty, since I've been doing this for more than a year now.

My friend Mona said to me one day, "I don't know how you keep thinking of things to write about."

The truth is, I don't know either. I find myself running out of ideas and I begin to panic. Then, out of the blue, something strikes me as funny, strange, annoying, precious, or just plain different, and I feel the need to comment.

Sometimes I tell my husband I'm short on ideas and he helps me brainstorm. Usually these sessions are good for three or four ideas, and I'll write them down in a notebook and then work my way through them, interrupting the list whenever I come up with something spontaneously.

Today, however, I am seriously out of ideas. I looked through old columns but nothing struck me there. I tried looking at the Newberry Observer but no idea popped up. I thought of writing yet another column about my garden but I'm guessing that people have heard enough on that subject and really don't care what I'm harvesting this week (tomatoes, cucumbers, and potatoes, since the borers took the squash plants) so that ruins that idea.

I searched through my calendar book and the little notebook in which I jot down the ideas and I'm just fresh out of luck.

The only things on those lists which I haven't addressed are "Mama's boys/Daddy's girls" and "funerals" and I'm not feeling especially knowledgeable about the differences between the South and West in those two areas. You see, I usually need a couple of anecdotes to build a column around and I don't have any for those two topics, thankfully!

I told my husband I was out of ideas and he suggested that I could quote the words for the entire song made famous by Groucho Marx which said, "I just came to say I must be going." Hmmm. not much help there!

So, here I am admitting that Miriam has nothing to say and doesn't know what to do about it. My husband suggests that those who know me will want to mark it on their calendars. In my own defense, I do come from a long line of storytellers. Storytelling. There's an idea for a column, but I think I used it already. Oh well.

I believe I've told you that my favorite Southernism is the one which you use when you don't know what to say. Since I've about reached my "word number goal" I'll go ahead and say it, Mmm, mmm, MMM, mmm . . .

And you could all respond with, "Well bless her heart, that girl's finally done run out of things to talk about!"

Oh wait! I just had an idea. I could write about mosquitoes. But I'm out of space. Guess I'll put it in the notebook for next week.

— 57 —

Bugs

Last evening I came out of the church to a cacophonic buzz that put a smile on my face. It was loud. It was mind numbing. It spoke the word "August" to me. It was locusts.

I felt like I was a child again, coming out of church on an August evening and walking the block to my house with the locusts buzzing. In those days — before air conditioners — the locusts were the background to my Daddy's message since the windows of the church were open to let the slightest breeze in. They were also the "white noise" I heard as I fell asleep.

One of the ladies at church commented on the cicadas. I hadn't heard them called that before, but she mentioned that they were louder than she had ever heard. They were loud, indeed.

A quieter but more cheerful little insect is the firefly — or as they are called here, lightning bugs. Coming from more arid land out west, I haven't had the opportunity to experience fireflies as much. The first time I remember seeing a firefly was in Athens, Georgia. I must have been about seven when we visited my Southern aunts and I saw the magical lights in the evening yard. It made us giggle and chase, dashing across the lawn doing our best to catch them.

Now, I love sitting on my porch or deck in North Carolina in the evening and watching the twinkling lights jump and sway across the yard and garden. I wish I could take some home in a jar this month for my nieces and nephews to see. I just don't think I want to talk my way through security at the airport with a jar of bugs. Besides, the fireflies would probably die on the way, and if not, they would die of thirst out there—wet year or not.

The firefly is preferable to the mosquito. It seems to me that the mosquitoes are so much bigger and more prolific here than they are out west. I suppose that is the humidity also. It's possible I just notice more because I have been out in the garden so many mornings and evenings.

I heard it's the girls that bite. They need the nutrition to make babies. Great . . . now my blood is feeding the future generations of mosquitoes. All the more reason to make sure they don't get to me. I hate spraying those chemicals on my skin, so I try to avoid them by going out when it is cool and breezy. I wear long sleeves and pants. I sometimes spray a big floppy hat to keep them away from my face.

I've also found that orange peels rubbed on my skin will help keep them away. Mosquitoes don't like oranges. That's another reason not to like mosquitoes.

In a couple of weeks I'll be heading to South Dakota. I'll let you know how the mosquitoes and locusts compare this year. Unfortunately, I'll have to wait until I get back home here to see fireflies.

— 58 —

Daddy's Girl

In a few days I'll fly out to South Dakota to see my family. It has been eight months and that is just too long – after about four months I start getting pitiful. But, scheduling and the price of travel have made me wait.

The only hard thing about getting married and moving down South was leaving my family. For ten years we all lived close except my youngest sister who was only six hours away. I saw my parents, siblings, nieces, and nephews at least every week. We were all there for each other and I never missed a birthday or other special event.

Then it ended. It was hard. But of course I was thrilled to be married.

Newberry reminds me of that time. I watch families who can have Sunday dinner together every week. I see families who can be there for each other in the hard times. I'm a little jealous sometimes.

But there is another side of that coin. My Daddy is an amazing man. I may seem to overstate his positive character qualities but, honestly, he is as wonderful as I say. That's a pretty hard thing for my husband to measure up to. And to be honest, it would have been harder if we had been right there with family— lovingly, of course—"all up in our business" as you say down here.

Being away from my family forced me to depend more on my husband, forced us to learn to stand together—just the two of us—and "cleave" as the Bible says.

But this difficult distance turned out to be a real gift. I have discovered my husband is even more amazing than I suspected when I married him. He is there for me, always (even checking every single column to make sure my commas are in the right place!)

I bring this up because of the Daddy's girl / Mama's boy thing that I see here. Some of it might come from the fact that people don't move away as much as out west. Or maybe, it is because the apron strings are longer here.

I don't know, but I definitely see a difference, especially in the Mamas and their sons. Here it is not unusual for a mom to be involved in helping her son handle business, fixing him lunches at her house, or doing other little things for him even when he has a wife. This is not the norm out west. Moms love their sons and feel anguish when they leave home, but getting them out the door and independent is their number one goal.

I don't know that it matters, but I find it interesting. I am impressed by the respect, appreciation, and care sons show their mothers here in the South.

I can tell you this. When I see my Daddy I'm going to hug his neck and be thankful for every moment I have with him. If that makes me a Daddy's girl, so be it.

— 59 —

Nothing Sweet About It

The other day I saw a status update on Facebook that made me chuckle. Then it grabbed me right in the gut. This is what it said: "Parting is such sweet sorrow. What a silly expression. I see nothing sweet about it."

I can certainly relate to that.

Like I said last week, when I got married it was hard to leave my family. When I got to Florida, though, the church people surrounded me with love, and I even had a nearby friend from college who shared her children with me any time I wanted. After only fifteen months I hated to say goodbye.

When we moved to Newberry neither of us had family here. Our closest family was a couple of hours away. However, I found substitutes of a sort for many of the people I was missing.

Our church family here became sisters and brothers. My co-workers here filled the void left by friends at work. One coworker and her husband became my new "Mom and Dad". Even now, I know that if I have a problem when Bruce is out of town, I have friends I can call. Our neighbors have been willing to watch our house, get our mail, and even let us enjoy hearing their children play in the yard.

The truth is, I found people to fill some of the void left by the move.

Whenever I move I'm always torn to bits at the thought of leaving all of these folks that I have come to love; but I have learned a lesson that has helped me over and over. It's the realization that I wouldn't be having a difficult time saying goodbye to these people if I had never left the last group. So, would I rather stay with these friends and forfeit the surety of a whole new batch? Not me! I like people.

What is Miriam rambling about today, you ask? Well, I'll quit beating around the bush and spit it out.

We are moving to Salisbury, North Carolina. We are excited about the new town, the history of the area, and new opportunities.

But my heart breaks. It means more goodbyes. It means that this weekly column will be ending today. I'm going to miss telling everyone in town what I think of things — that's been kind of fun. I'm going to miss my walks up Main Street and back home. I'm going to miss our church and the friends I've made.

Despite the difficulty of leaving, I'm choosing to remember this: I'm not just saying goodbye to old friends, I'm saying hello to the possibility of new ones.

If you want to keep up with my future thoughts or ramblings, you can check out my blogs. I have two, one for my books and one for my personal writings. They can be found at *www.doublecousins.wordpress.com*, or *www.miriamjonesbradley.com*.

We'll be in and out for a bit yet, and I plan to be at Oktoberfest. Maybe I'll see you there! If not, there's one more thing I want you to know. I may not be from here, but I'll always think of Newberry as a place I love and was blessed to call home.

— 60 —
The Last Word

Editor's Note: I asked Miriam what her strongest memories or impressions were of her year of writing a weekly column. Here are her answers to the question.

The biggest benefit turned out to be finding her "voice", her authentic style of expression, which is something that takes time and practice to develop. Before taking on the column, she had written her first children's mystery, but that drew heavily on family experiences, and it was more, in a way, giving voice to her family and childhood and less to the adult she has become.

A parallel benefit was how much she learned about herself in the process. The columns focus, obviously, on her perceptions and understandings, and it is sometimes quite a challenge to put those into words: before they can be verbalized, they have to be recognized and understood.

A second parallel benefit would be how much she learned about the South. She has always been interested in history, especially if it is told as a story about people. Now she has had the perfect excuse to dig into local and regional history and the perfect laboratory to test her new insights. That "research" for the column was pure fun.

And, of course, there were the technical aspects of writing. She says that the column gig came at just the right time with respect to improving and polishing her writing skills—"such a gift" was how she expressed it. With practice, writers grow not only in their powers of expression but also in the more mundane skills of choosing the right words, writing more concisely, using better grammar and punctuation, and becoming better self editors.

Always one to rise to the challenge of a deadline, over the year of the column, she developed habits of making notes of ideas for future work, learned to pace her writing so it seldom caused a last minute rush, and learned to write more quickly. In short, she became an overall much better writer.

Finally, two side benefits not directly or even indirectly related to the writing process: first, the connections she made in the community because of the column. There is quite possibly no other way she could have become so much a part of Newberry in such a short time as publicly sharing of herself in the newspaper. And, second, the column, along with the book(s), provided a springboard into speaking in schools about the writing process. As Miriam has grown as a writer, she has delighted in sharing those lessons with students.

— C. Bruce Bradley, editor, May 2015

ABOUT THE AUTHOR

Miriam Jones Bradley was born in Castro Valley, California, while her dad was in seminary. She grew up in California, Nebraska, and Wyoming, went to college in Wisconsin as an adult, and landed in South Dakota. So when she married a Southerner and moved South, there were some — several — okay, a *lot* of cultural adjustments.

She is a Registered Nurse and also has a degree in Elementary Education, which she applies in her speaking at schools.

She now lives in Western North Carolina with her husband, Bruce.

The *Double Cousins Mystery* series continues, with the fourth book due out in early Fall 2015. A new series featuring *The Nearly Twins*, and set in various Southern locations, is set to debut in Spring of 2016.

The author can be contacted through her website at *www.MiriamJonesBradley.com* or at *MiriamJonesBradley@gmail.com*.

PHOTO AND IMAGE CREDITS

Front Cover

Back Cover

Avenue of Oaks, Spring Hill College, Mobile, Alabama
http://commons.wikimedia.org/wiki/File:4307_Old_Shell_Road_Stewartf
Public Domain by copyright holder's release.

Page 3: Photo and byline in the Newberry Observer. Used by permission.

Page 4: First headline for the column in the Newberry Observer. Used by permission.

Page 13: Newberry's Pork in the Park festival, April 2008: Photo by C. Bruce Bradley; used by permission. All other rights reserved.

Page 14: Old Courthouse. Creative Commons image referenced above for the front cover.

INDEX